CORPORATE REHAB

Cheering you on!

Jennie

CORPORATE REHAB

Ditch the hustle culture
and thrive again

JENNIE BLUMENTHAL

Corporate Rehab: *Ditch the hustle culture and thrive again*

Copyright © 2022 by Jennie Blumenthal

Jones Media Publishing
10645 N. Tatum Blvd. Ste. 200-166
Phoenix, AZ 85028
www.JonesMediaPublishing.com

Disclaimer:
The author strives to be as accurate and complete as possible in the creation of this book, notwithstanding the fact that he does not warrant or represent at any time that the contents within are accurate due to the rapidly changing nature of the Internet.

While all attempts have been made to verify information provided in this publication, the Publisher assumes no responsibility for errors, omissions, or contrary interpretation of the subject matter herein. Any perceived slights of specific persons, peoples, or organizations are unintentional.

In practical advice books, like anything else in life, there are no guarantees of income made. Readers are cautioned to reply on their own judgment about their individual circumstances to act accordingly. This book is not intended for use as a source of legal, business, accounting or financial advice. All readers are advised to seek services of competent professionals in legal, business, accounting, and finance field.

ISBN: 978-1-948382-44-1 paperback

Printed in the United States of America

For every woman who shared her story in these pages, and for those who carry their stories by themselves. You are not alone.

For Jackson and Avery, for holding up a mirror when I needed it most, and reminding me that I know myself best.

And for Kevin, for leaping with me into the unknown, and for every day that came after.

***

What is the greatest lesson a woman should learn?
That since day one
She's already had everything she needs within herself
It's the world that convinced her she did not

—rupi kaur

***

TABLE OF CONTENTS

INTRODUCTION

"Tell me, what is it you plan to do with your one wild and precious life?

— Mary Oliver

I am not the person you imagine when you think of *addiction*. You might breathe a sigh of relief that, in the word addiction, I must be talking about drugs or alcohol; this doesn't apply to you, right? But hear me out. If addiction is really any behavior that becomes compulsive, despite harmful consequences, that sounds an awful lot like the cycle I was trapped in. A vague feeling of being unfulfilled, despite racking up work accomplishments. Trapped in a cycle of wanting to do more in my life, with success as a near-enemy—where the more I worked, the more the validation flowed. It was easier to check more things off my list and feel that small hit of accomplishment (or more accurately, dopamine) than to deal with the real feelings of exhaustion, burnout, loneliness, and confusion, wondering if I was spending my days on Earth doing what I was truly *meant* to be doing.

Where the more of myself I threw into the job, the less of my *real* self remained. After twenty years of *appearing* fulfilled by my constant hustling, I decided to break my addiction– to my job, my accomplishments, and all the validation that came with these things. Instead, I'd build a life I could enjoy.

I will tell you my story, the moment I realized I was addicted, and my journey out of a life I had been merely surviving and into a life where I am now thriving. My hope is that, if you find yourself in a similar space, you'll now have a roadmap showing you where to go next.

In the few years leading up to this, I found myself boarding more and more planes– at least a few days a week. I'd justify time away from my husband and two elementary schoolers as a means for my children to see their mom doing what she loved; I was a strong woman they could look up to, right? Bringing in an income and supporting the family had turned into breadwinning and earning enough for nice vacations. The phone would ring and I'd be on a plane to the next place where my assistance was needed—always the fixer, responding to urgent requests rather than setting my own agenda. In my twenty-year tenure, I ran multi-million dollar business units and government technology programs, managed teams across Europe and Asia, and presented to teams and C-suites across multiple cities per week. My calendar was filled in thirty-minute blocks from eight a.m. to eight p.m., at which point I'd switch to entertaining clients if I was on the road, or try to re-engage with my family for a mere two hours of dinner, homework, and life management if I was home.

Some days hung together with duct tape, handing off kid schedules, dividing and conquering with our nanny and my surgeon husband, while he worked his own 50-hour weeks. Weeks no longer felt productive and neatly arranged—they were a 100 mile per hour sprint until Friday, when things still weren't complete, but it was socially unacceptable to keep working, and a glass of wine was my reward for finishing another week of activity.

Then a global pandemic hit. Planes were grounded, distractions were gone. I was forced to take a long hard look at my life. The pace continued to be grueling, complete with twelve-hour days, toggling between running a company business unit and troubleshooting online school for my kids. I found a ton of newfound purpose in leading my team at work to build innovative solutions to help our clients save their jobs, as the travel industry was in freefall. At home, we took up tennis as a family, and I traded time in airports for dinners by the pool. Thinking I had maybe finally figured out a work/life balance, I turned to my son one morning in late August and said, "I know you missed your elementary school graduation and this pandemic has been terrible for so many, but I feel like we've gotten a lot of great family time this summer." He enthusiastically and honestly responded, "Yeah, that was so great! I mean, you were still on Zoom calls for, like, 12 hours every day, but I got to see you on the weekends!"

And that did it. Something inside me cracked open. Or broke. Maybe it was the façade I was working so hard to uphold—that I was "happy." That this was what I *wanted*. What I had worked so hard for.

Suddenly, I let myself ask the questions I had been running from: *Why was I doing this job? Is this the relationship I wanted with my husband? How could I justify being away from my kids so much and not being an active participant in their world...all to show them how great a work ethic is? If I was going to be honest with myself...was I even really doing it for them? Or was I proving something to myself?* In an environment where I would never be enough, I would never do enough, I would never have enough to be able to comfortably stop. I looked at the senior leadership team of my company and it hit me: they didn't just have jobs I didn't want, they had *lives* I didn't want. Each one had plenty of money and power. But most were divorced, or estranged from their kids, or still traveling weekly, well into their fifties. If I was pointing my star towards them, what made me think I was going to end up differently?

So I resigned. Without a plan. Without a next step. When I left, I told my boss, "I don't know what I will do next, I just know it's *not* this." When you leave to prioritize your children, it's hard for someone to criticize, so I realize I had a bit of a shield around my decision and the privilege to be able to make it. But the reality was that I was leaving to prioritize me, and my family, amidst a system that would never make that tradeoff. If I had stayed, I would have prioritized the fulfillment I got at work, at the expense of everything else. And if the quality of life is the quality of your relationships—with others, for sure—but especially with yourself... *how could I stay?*

I was confident in my decision and clear for the first time in a long time. Fifty people wanted to have thirty-minute phone calls to understand– from Partner Affairs, to junior staff, to fellow partners. I seemed to have it all, so what happened? What had I discovered that they could avoid, or else distance themselves from, to stay safe knowing that their decisions to stay in the job were the right ones? As I explained my desire to reconnect with my husband and kids and live a full life, and my disillusionment with some aspects of our corporate strategy – which had increasingly become a death march to higher share prices – every single person I spoke with told me in hushed tones that they wished they could make a similar choice. Every. Single. One.

Not one colleague or client told me, "Wow, I'm really happy and fulfilled, and I can't imagine why you're not." But many did tell me, almost as a confession to a departing colleague or business partner who couldn't hold it against them or tell anyone else, that they had waited too long, or they had built up such a lifestyle that this job was the only way they could afford it or pay for college, or that they had sacrificed their health and believed they lost five years of their lifespan, or their husbands weren't breadwinners and they felt they couldn't leave, or their spouse had just left them and they figured they should throw themselves further into their careers. Most had a similar sad story, framed as he or she not having a choice. Many of them went on to take even larger jobs in the same companies after the pandemic, and I wonder if they were honest with themselves. Did they realize they just doubled down on their own despair? But a few told me, "You are lucky; you're getting out." One even said, "You need to write a book about this so that others know they have choices."

To understand what led to my decision, and the work I had to do after I left, I needed to understand why I had *stayed*. Which decisions had been helpful for a point in my career, but weren't fully re-evaluated as my needs changed, and as I grew. In trying to understand what had kept me hooked, I began to unravel the decisions that had overstayed their welcome. Reaching way back into my past, I had grandparents who had survived the Great Depression and fought in wars, teaching me and my sister that financial security through education and a good job meant having *options*. And options meant *survival*. My parents had each suffered loss early in life; the pain never fully healed, the losses seldom discussed. When something was hard, we leaned on our Irish roots and kept our heads down, applied grit or ambition and, rather than digging into the pain, we looked on the bright side. We gave ourselves no permission to rest, or to consider quitting– ever. Having options to avoid pain became the main lens through which all other decisions were filtered. Back then, we couldn't have known that processing pain and learning the language of emotion was a crucial part of just being human.

When I graduated college, dated my husband long distance, and later put him through medical residency for seven years on a meager salary, that self-reliance and grit came in handy. I was alone a lot, and poor time boundaries around work were the first thing to go. One boss complimented my ability to stay focused and tune out detractors and distractions by saying, "it's like you have blinders on." Those blinders kept me coming back to work full-time after each maternity leave, and always staying the course when two careers and two babies became overwhelming. *"I'll stay on this track until I can't do it anymore,"* I would say to myself, *"and then I'll walk away."* Earn myself options. In a male-dominated company, I watched female colleagues have babies, come back and get paid for part-time, but wind up working full-time hours, and then eventually quit, dismissed by male colleagues as "not being able to hack it." That's a convenient way to boil down a complicated set of family and career decisions to a lens of: do it our way, or you're not enough. I was not going to admit failure, or allow myself to rest. I pressed on and, for career advancement and financial security, it worked.

But something isn't working for women in corporate America today. Women are dropping out of the workforce at alarming rates—accelerated by the pressures of the Covid pandemic. Nearly 50 million people quit their jobs in 2021 during what has been termed the Great Resignation, or Great Re-Evaluation, with women making up 100% of the workers who left in December 2020.[1] C. Nicole Mason, President and Chief Executive of the Institute for Women's Policy Research, coined the term she-cession, questioning whether women's advancement in the workplace was just set back by twenty years. While Covid was a catalyst for many, there is a more complex set of underlying factors, namely: record levels of burnout, high self-expectations, few role models, and

---

[1] *Interactive Chart: How Historic Has the Great Resignation Been?* (SHRM, March 9, 2022)

lack of support structures for childcare. Combined, these immerse women in a perfect storm of feeling that there are few good options.

I interviewed over 300 women for this book to see if my story stood alone, and a theme began to emerge from the discussions: women wanted *more* from their lives. Women in today's workplace were raised to believe they could have it all. The big career, the close-knit family, the active social life, the downtime and relaxation. I, however, believe we were sold the promise of a dream house without any blueprints. We had few role models helping us to navigate what *having it all* at work and at home could mean for each of us, and what tradeoffs would be required. It was an ideal forged by legions of women who just wanted a seat at the table, and fought for their daughters to be anything, to be able to do it all. They couldn't have known what it would require in those organizations because very few actually made it.

This mindset placed all the responsibility on the woman, ignoring realities of systemic impediments to reach the C-suite. You can do it all. Just lean in *further*. If you don't make it, that's on you.

That mentality leaves out the reality of what it takes to succeed in corporate America, or healthcare, education, non-profits, and government, judging by the stories of the hundreds of women I interviewed. It forgets the reality of the homes we grew up in that shaped us and our worldview, which we then carried into the workplace. It omits the reality of the American workforce being the only developed country lacking modern support for workers in childcare options, eldercare, and paid leave.[2] And it ignores the realities of discrimination, sexual assault, and lack of diversity—themes echoed in the women's stories I gathered.

---

[2] Gretchen Livingston and Deja Thomas. *Among 41 countries, only the U.S. lacks paid parental leave* (Pew Research Center, December 16, 2019).

Maybe some executive women think they want to be in the C-suite; they want to be Jeff Bezos, minus the phallic rocket. Plus, have a family or full life outside of work. The equation in their mind is that if they reach the executive ranks, then they will have made it, and they can finally exhale and have it all. But I don't think they realize how difficult that dream is to maintain. They aren't fully informed about the tradeoffs required to reach that level and how easy it can be to lose yourself along the way, or how to actually stop and enjoy their lives when they reach the pinnacle. How to really grow as a person alongside the growth of your career. *How could they? Who can they look to as an example? Do they even feel like they have choices once they begin down this path?*

I'm here to tell you: we were never meant to do it *all*. We were meant to be fully ourselves. There is no blueprint for a successful female executive with a robust family and social life, but we're building it right now. This is the first generation of women who have more skillsets and financial means than their mothers. Women who have paid their dues, rising up the ranks, and reaching a point where they can afford the privilege of having *choices*. Against this backdrop, a global pandemic ushered in a collective rise in consciousness, prompting many of us to think hard about these choices and tradeoffs. To chase happiness alongside success. To define what success even means for you. To take leadership of your own life.

Doing it "all" will certainly cost you. But the conclusion is not to be less; it's to be *more* in the ways that are meaningful to you. It's time to reconnect to yourself. To brush away the things that helped you cope, that got you here, and kept you running so hard for so long. It's time to make intentional choices, fully informed by data and tradeoffs, and be open to changing them as you evolve. Part of the reason I am called to write this book is to help the countless others who've shared their stories with me and are eager for a way to find a path to a whole life while avoiding the pitfalls and traps. I owe it to them, and I owe it to my children's generation. A legion of girls who see their exhausted mothers, anxious about missing camp sign-ups or not having enough #MakingMemories posts on Facebook. Mothers who are desperate to get off the corporate treadmill, but dying under the weight of expectations that they raise their daughters with the right work ethic. Women dying on the hill of doing it all...because deep down, we feel we are not enough.

I believe we have always been enough. There are multiple paths for success, and it is up to each of us to constantly redefine what that looks like, making intentional choices based on these tradeoffs and adjusting as necessary. The reality is that we're making these choices today while deeply disconnected from ourselves.

There are many factors at play: limiting beliefs based on our past, the false dichotomy of work versus life, the intoxicating pull of the hustle culture and the shiny validation it offers, the actual real demands and responsibilities of caretaking, the pain from wounds we'd rather not acknowledge, the information imbalance with employers, toxic corporate cultures or managers, and the feeling that you do not have a choice.

One way to reconnect to yourself, determine your path, and make intentional choices – and the way I did that for myself – is to put yourself through your own corporate rehab. I broke my addiction to the hustle culture and rebuilt my life. After I left, I'd like to say I never looked back. Instead, I spent the following year looking back on the last forty. As the pandemic wore on and I found myself with some time to think, without the constant rush of kids running out the door to school, emails pinging and calls to jump on, I began to ask myself the questions I usually pushed away. I consumed everything I could to understand this new phase I was suddenly in and to name the feelings I was having around loss of identity and seeing repeating patterns. I'd jokingly tell friends it felt like

I was putting myself through detox and rehab from my corporate mindset. And the name stuck.

I began pulling apart my thoughts, feelings and choices and how they had formed over time, asking myself, *what decisions did I make that landed me here in a self-imposed prison, when I actually thought I was happy? What in my past conditioning led me to make these decisions, some consciously, and many not? Which choices were based on other people's actions, manipulating my options often for what they believed was my own good? What part of it was circumstances driven by toxic cultures in corporate America, and how can we go about changing those? Why did the job suddenly become unfulfilling?*

I tried to answer the question Mary Oliver asks, which had called out to me from a place deep within, from an inscription I came across years ago: *Tell me, what is it you plan to do with your one wild and precious life?*

These questions are the focus of this book: to help you separate from the hustle culture, reconnect with yourself, change your own self-leadership, and then change the teams and structures around you. You can take the girl out of corporate, but you can't make her give up a whiteboard, a laptop, and a good old framework to define and solve a problem. After building my own approach to break the cycle of addiction to hustle culture and the corporate mentality, I began sharing what I had learned with women who were asking themselves similar questions. I summarized my insights, research, and approach into the Corporate Rehab leadership framework© and began to work with executive women and entrepreneurs, helping them lead at a higher level without losing themselves in the process. The need was so great that I began to brainstorm ways to help more women beyond coaching, and the idea of this book was born. I wound up interviewing 300 executive women, because storytelling is a way for us to really see ourselves and the patterns we are living through others. As I listened to heart-wrenching tales, several similar themes emerged. I was not alone. To enable me to let these women tell you their truth, all names and companies have been anonymized. And, now, I want to share this approach and their stories with you. I hope this book will help you recognize yourself in its pages, examine some of your own behaviors and mindsets, determine if there are patterns to drop or healing to be done, and then grow and build a life that is more authentically yours.

While we are talking about you, for the purposes of this book, the term "woman" refers to people who identify with presenting as female, though I recognize this is a varied group. While my stories are that of a hardworking yet still privileged cis white woman, wife, and mother, the hundreds of women I interviewed came from multiple ethnicities, orientations, and marital statuses, though mostly from the professional class and are likely in similar socio-economic standing. I'll acknowledge that there are so many parts of identity – race, gender, class, ethnicity, orientation, ability, roles – that I felt I couldn't possibly give enough weight to each equally, but I want to acknowledge and honor their stories just the same.

The caregiver who is childless by choice but responsible for an adult parent. The gay, Latina woman who is united with others on women's equality, yet suffers pay and privilege inequities. The black consultant who was asked not to attend a client meeting at a country club, for fear she would be shunned and her white colleagues wouldn't know how to handle it. The successful neurodiverse executive who is consistently underestimated, and uses that to her advantage to help other employees gain leverage where she can. The stay-at-home mom whose choice to leave the workforce was never meant to be permanent, and is now ready for more but not interested in 60-hour workweeks. The breadwinner or the single mother who doesn't have the luxury to quit, let alone time to dream about her purpose.

It is my hope that these insights and stories help you to accept the things you cannot change in your world, like other people's responses, but find the courage to change the things you can, from how you show up, to your ability to fight for all to have the same rights and opportunities.

If rehabilitation is really the process of restoring something to its former condition or health, that's exactly what we'll focus on in this book: reconnecting to lost parts of yourself so you can make intentional decisions for yourself and those you lead. For forty years I navigated expertly with my head; in this book, I've added the navigation tool I wish I'd listened to long ago: the compass of my *heart*. To appeal to your logic, I included academic studies and research where possible, and turned to primary research through my own and the women's stories I collected to emphasize key points and appeal to your heart. We'll begin by examining how we get lost in the first place, how the hustle culture becomes a convenient trap for both individuals and organizations, and the making of identity. Next, we'll step through the Corporate Rehab leadership framework© to truly REHAB:

- Recognize your life's story
- Evaluate patterns and relationships
- Heal your mind, body and spirit
- Arise and reconnect with yourself and your strengths, and
- Build new dimensions of your career and life.

Along the way, you'll find exercises and a roadmap to begin your own rehab. Finally, a call to action for a better way for leaders.

Let's get started.

CHAPTER 1

HUSTLING FOR OUR WORTH

"You either walk inside your story and own it or you stand outside your story and hustle for your worthiness."

— Brene Brown

It was a Tuesday morning, the first day back after Labor Day, when I resigned from my twenty-year corporate career. The façade had cracked, and I finally admitted to myself that this job was slowly killing me. Before that, things had seemingly been going really well. I had worked hard, been admitted to the partnership five years prior, pulled in big deals, had earned the respect of my clients and colleagues, and had just proven myself as the only woman on our business unit's leadership team. I was on an upward track; well-positioned to take on a big new job.

But that was all on the surface. Beneath it, in a place I didn't like to think about, I had known my spirit was slowly dying. With the pace I kept, I worried I would have a heart attack or develop cancer; in a twisted way, thinking the only thing that could get me off this corporate treadmill was to have another baby, or to get sick. I worried I didn't invest enough time in my relationship with my husband or my kids. I was physically there when I wasn't on the road; I attended all the events and sang them to sleep when home, before knocking out a few more emails. But I was often distracted, turning myself into a pretzel, trying to conform into an all-in-one executive and invested mother. I received so much validation from work; the constant pull of emails and meetings and accomplishments was an easy hit that kept on giving. I told myself that, because I was successful, I was *happy*. Someone or something had to force me to change because I was too stuck in the mindset to make a change myself. I was too stuck to even realize I was making a choice about how I spent my time and what got my attention. *Like an addict.*

The women I interviewed shared similar stories of hustle and overwork. Barb, a COO turned yoga instructor, told me she knew something was wrong the day she raced between calls to get a lunch she could devour mindlessly, and passed out, her head crashing through the drywall in the kitchen. Amy confided she was losing sleep, her schedule packed with international travel and high expectations and, in her distraction, she didn't notice her teenage daughter's increasing problems with bullies at school. Cassie, an IT contractor, locked herself in her office and couldn't stop crying. Several women told me that they *thought* they were happy, right up to the moment that their brothers or husbands pulled them aside and told them that they were always rushing, always working, always *angry*.

Women are exhausted and overwhelmed, and we are addicted. To the pace of the hustle culture, to our jobs, to the identity that comes with them, and sometimes to the toxic culture that produces them. As Brigid Schulte writes in her book, aptly titled *Overwhelmed*, "...this is how it feels to live my life: scattered, fragmented, and exhausting."[3] The people who lead companies and set the tone

---

[3] Brigid Schulte, *Overwhelmed: How to Work, Love and Play When Nobody Has Time.* (Picador, 2015)

often have unhealed wounds themselves, or have traded off parts of their humanity for financial security and encourage the same tradeoffs in the cultures they reign over. To both survive this scenario and learn to thrive in your life, you need to recognize and escape this mindset.

I worked as a partner for a large firm, and consulted for many Fortune 500 companies all over the world and across sectors including consumer products, telecom, travel, government, academia, and non-profit. I've presented in boardrooms from Manhattan to Dubai, counseling CEOs on Park Avenue and running million dollar technology programs from server rooms. I've seen it all and, yet, I still found myself shocked as women I interviewed detailed horrific abuse and toxic cultures that excused it away. Many had never told their stories to anyone. There were days I had to decompress from what I'd heard. Other stories were of ordinary moments when a woman realized she had lost herself in her role. But all were situations that included unhealthy behaviors, or things that weren't good for the women involved. If we are talking about being rehabilitated, *what* exactly are we addicted to?

It's **the hustle culture**. In her New York Times article, Erin Griffith defines *hustle culture* as that expectation to constantly be on the go, working without a pause, and turning every activity into productivity.[4] It glorifies overwork, and thrives on an environment of fear. It should be noted that this is different from hustle or grit, which we all need from time to time. The hustle culture is a *constant* pattern where you are "on" all the time; you don't give yourself the necessary pauses, constantly checking emails or hopping to and from social events. It applies just as easily to a corporate executive

---

[4] Erin Griffith, *Why Are Young People Pretending to Love Work?* (NY Times, Jan 26, 2019)

obsessively checking email, as it does to a stay-at-home mom who is doing all the things and documenting every move on Facebook. It shows up in a multitude of ways. Fear of missing out (FOMO), by needing to attend all the parties, volunteer opportunities, and business trips so that you don't get left behind. Over-identifying with your job or your role, where you can get a sense of validation and overworking to feel needed, and more of your identity becomes about your career. And, as a result, losing meaningful connected time with loved ones, or neglecting ourselves, to keep up with work and life demands.

Hustle culture can show up as an executive who doesn't protest additional assignments or trips because they feel a sense of importance at work, where they are revered or, at least, respected. Their corporate identity begins to overshadow the rest of their roles in life, sometimes leading to shallow relationships with their spouse or children - and often they are adrift in retirement. It could be the stay-at-home mom who feels so connected to her role as a mother, that she loses herself in her children's lives, forgetting about the dreams she had for herself and feeling more fulfillment by living through her children's experiences and turning to social media to get the connection she is missing. It could be one of the several female executives who confided she knew she should *want* to be home with her kids, but she was so tired of doing it all; the idea of just one business trip where nobody needed her, where she could enjoy uninterrupted sleep in a room someone else would clean, was nothing short of *intoxicating*.

And the more insidious form is when the hustle culture creeps into the crevices of your life and takes hold; you're making decisions without fully knowing it, until something jars you awake. Jill, a consultant in her 30s climbing the corporate ladder, told me she knew exactly what she needed to do to reach the next level but, once she reached it, suddenly found herself questioning how she got there and if she even liked it. "It was easy to get through life when I identified with my work," Jill said, "and I don't have to ask the hard questions; it becomes easy to evaluate whether I have time for things when I only use one lens: work."

Hustle culture can look like over-scheduling nights and weekends and never really having downtime to rest or recharge. If you keep running, maybe you don't have to deal with pesky or painful thoughts and feelings. It could be in hoarding money, by working more hours long after you have enough to support your lifestyle. For the men I interviewed, work was an easy numbing device to not have to deal with the reality of raising small kids or feeling unfulfilled at work, or at home. For many of the women I interviewed, their numbing device was Netflix. It could be chemical addictions, like those found in alcohol, drugs, or cigarettes. But it could just as easily be the serotonin and dopamine, which mimic natural high, that keep you scrolling late night on social media.[5]

The distraction of the urgent keeps you hooked. It prevents you from listening to that little voice that knows you're not meant for this. But when your calendar is full of meetings from 8 am to 8 pm, and you operate your life by packing in as much as you can, it conveniently allows you to not have to listen. That voice is different for each of us, but it is usually telling us that something in our lives needs our attention. It could be pain from old wounds, a disconnect in how you're spending your time and what you profess to value, a relationship that needs attention, or a calling to a different purpose in your life or work. The stories of the women I spoke with tell me that if we try to drown it out, it only gets louder. Distraction or numbing through the ways mentioned above is

[5] Trevor Haynes, *Dopamine, Smartphones & You: A battle for your time* (Harvard, May 1 2018)

effective; it prevents us from having to actually *feel*. But our bodies are designed to do just that: feel for signals. From you, to you.

"When I'm very busy, I don't have time to think about what I want...so I don't have to think about my own choices very much."

The hustle culture is rooted in a scarcity mentality. There's not enough time, money, attention, or resources; someone else may get there first if you don't hurry or perform well. When you've experienced this mentality, either in yourself or from the guidance of a meaningful role model in your life, it can impact your decisions long after the threat of scarcity has gone. Hustle culture and this scarcity is deeply ingrained in our culture, as most of us came from somewhere else, and had to work hard to achieve the *American Dream*. That grit and determination could earn you whatever lifestyle you wanted. It impacts what we value, how we view our own self-worth, our relationship with productivity, our definitions of success, the amount of vacation or relaxation we allow ourselves to take, and how hard we push ourselves. When we are in a scarcity mindset, we make decisions in survival mode. We hustle for our worth outside of ourselves. We believe it is the only way to feel we are enough. The hustle culture says you need to perform well in order to be deemed worthy. It reminds me of the time a boss tried to make my colleague, a new father, get back on the road the same week his daughter was born. When I mentioned we should try to find a local assignment for him instead, our boss responded, "Well, how is he going to pay for college for her if he doesn't get back on the road?" She was four days old.

Of course, the opposite of a scarcity mentality is an *abundance* mentality. You have enough, you are doing enough, and you are already enough just based on having been born. You can permit yourself to relax and read a book instead of rushing to fit in the laundry or a social event so you don't feel you are missing out. You can drive your team to outsized financial returns, while balancing decisions that permit them to rebound from sprints of activity, like forced vacation time, emails returned within normal working hours, and setting stretch goals but not unrealistic ones. Some of it is literally all in our heads. When you approach the day like a race to get it all done, and get that deal or that coveted parking spot before the competition, your brain is already activating survival mode. When you approach the day expecting that things will go well, that you will complete the most important tasks, that there will be enough time, and you will attract the right clients or deals, you're telling your brain that you're operating in abundance mode. *There is enough.* It changes the way you show up in the world, and the people and situations you attract based on that energy. Calm, focused, and driven. Or frenzied, hurried, and fearful. Open or closed.

The hustle culture is so addictive because it distracts us from connecting with ourselves. Instead of examining our mindset to see whether we are open or closed, we rush to achieve a goal or finish the laundry. Instead of stopping to see how your body itself is responding in a situation, we numb what is coming up because we don't have the capacity or time or emotional skills to handle it. Instead of asking yourself whether this career or role is something you actually want, you rush to climb the ladder, hoping security and fulfillment are waiting for you at the top.

"When the goal isn't to outperform your parents' generation, your choices become different. You get to be more intentional about how you spend your time and resources."

Staying busy keeps us from stopping to ask what we are feeling, thinking, and doing– from being truly aware of our mindsets and behaviors. If we did stop and reconnect with ourselves, we may be forced to evaluate whether the situations we are in are truly good for us. Whether they are meeting our true needs, or whether we are allowing an addiction to the hustle culture to serve as a cheap substitute. Maslow's Hierarchy of Needs arranges all human needs into an ascending order, from basic bodily needs like safety and security, to mental and spiritual needs like connection and belonging, esteem and respect, and finally self-actualization as you move up the pyramid. In my research and interviews, I found **the hustle culture keeps us distracted from meeting our human needs of security, connection, esteem, and purpose**.

Security

I believe the hustle culture attracts people who have had some experience with life in survival mode. When you are in survival mode, you have been exposed to things that emphasize basic needs: financial security, dominance, safety. This can loosely translate to a title, a salary, or making it to the top of your profession, so that you can avoid ever having to feel vulnerable. It's easy for your mind to dip back into survival mode when a new perceived threat arises: a recession, a job loss, instability in relationships at home. And when you are surviving, there's less room for thriving: creative innovation, giving up some power to make growth possible for more of your colleagues, or actually rewarding humane work cultures.

When you make your decisions with a heavily skewed financial implication, often the human side of that debate loses. It made me wonder: is humane just the opposite of hustle culture? Are executives ever forced to think about those tradeoffs in the moment, like should we drive more profit, or allow more breaks in the day for workers? Should we hire more teachers and fund them appropriately, or should we just expect them to do more even though we are giving them less? In this case, the survival mentality exists from corporate and medical to education settings and beyond.

Careers can help give us security, connection, esteem, and purpose– there's nothing wrong with that. The problem becomes when we give a role more power and weight in our lives than we intended; we look to the roles we play to meet the *majority* of these needs. And it can happen in your role as a marketing executive or as a mother. The hustle culture doesn't care whether you're in a business suit or a bathing suit at any given moment.

Connection

Once our basic needs are met, the next level of need is connection. Yet in our world today, there is a growing disconnection from ourselves, from our purpose, and from each other. And, as we become more *digitally* connected, we are ever hungrier for authentic connection. Social psychologist Sherry Turkle argues in her book, *Alone Together*, that our constant connection to the digital world is driving isolation: we are now "more lonely and distant from one another...this is not only changing the way we interact online, it's straining our personal relationships, as well."[6] As humans, we are hardwired to belong and to connect with others. In his book, *Social Intelligence: The New Science of Human Relationships*, Daniel Goleman shares research stating that we are hardwired for connection, both within our biology and our brains, and this is impacted by both experiences and relationships. And if we aren't getting our needs for connection and purpose met, sometimes we'll attempt to get them in unhealthy ways.[7]

---

[6] Sherry Turkle, *Alone Together* (New York, Basic Books, 2012)
[7] Brené Brown, As referenced in *The Gifts of Imperfection: Let Go of Who You Think You're Supposed to Be and Embrace Who You Are* (Hazelden Foundation, 2010).

I realized only in hindsight that as the kids got older and devices replaced tummy time, we hadn't built enough downtime into our weeks to really connect as a family. Teens who rolled their eyes as I yelled for them to put shoes on or put down the phone as we rushed out the door to sporting events provided a stark contrast to being thought of as smart and interesting for my ideas in a pitch at work. In one role, I was a drag. In the other, I was respected. It wasn't a real connection, but it did feel validating. But if we don't really spend the time understanding who we are - our dreams, our needs, our motivations, our limiting beliefs we may not even be aware of - how can we connect authentically with others? Sometimes we aren't able to give the best of ourselves because we don't even know who that is. And as we grow, how do we stay in touch with who we are, even as our priorities shift?

Esteem

Self-esteem can sometimes be translated into significance or validation; wanting to be seen and heard. Depending on your background and intentions, work can bring meaning to our lives, it can afford your children basic needs or a certain lifestyle, it can provide a sense of pride as we identify with the value that we bring into the outside world, and it can make us feel needed or wanted. None of these things are bad in themselves - the challenge lies when people, unaware of their motivations, align their self-esteem too closely with the role they are filling at this phase in their lives. Translating the value they bring into the world into mere dollars and cents, or worse— how much praise and value *other* people assign to their efforts.

 "I don't want my daughter to need the level of validation from others that I did."

Sarah, a media executive turned entrepreneur, recalls the validation she received in her corporate role as being "the fixer." It was so gratifying to be the youngest female senior vice president in the company's history, able to solve other people's office dilemmas all day long. It made her feel truly needed. The only catch? She was a single mom with a newborn at home, and the schedule she had to keep to maintain her work persona of fixing things, knowing the answers, and always being "on," kept her tethered to a work identity that wasn't actually working for her. We all need validation. The key is becoming aware of how you're receiving it.

Purpose

When our other needs are met, focusing on purpose or self-actualization is the final stage in the evolution of you becoming the best version of yourself. Purpose is your reason for being. It can get us in a state of flow at work, or make us feel more connected to others and part of something larger than ourselves. It can give meaning to our lives. Viktor Frankl's famous book, *Man's Search for Meaning*, describes his time in concentration camps during the Second World War, and how those who had something to live for survived, while those who could not tie their daily existence to some sort of purpose lost the will to live.[8] The current trend of companies to better articulate their purpose has helped employees feel better about the work they do; but to feel personally fulfilled, make sure you tie your *personal* purpose to your company's mission in some way.

 "So often women look at life purpose as separate from work purpose, but really where you find most joy and fulfillment is where you can align these two."

---

[8] Viktor Frankl, *Man's Search for Meaning* (Vienna, 1946).

This is undoubtedly the topic I get asked about the most from my executive clients, though it is often framed as "trying to figure out what I want to do" and can be buried under layers of disillusionment, burnout, and boredom. For the women I coach, I noticed similar themes coming up when discussing purpose: the embarrassment of not knowing theirs, the confusion between why and how, and conflating a role with a purpose. First, there was a lot of pressure to figure out what they wanted to do and to do that quickly. One consultant, Priya, lamented the fact that she wanted to figure out what she really wanted during each of her maternity leaves, but there had been no time to think. Second, when discussing purpose or what lights them up, they'd move quickly from the "why" they are passionate about something, straight to the practical "what" that role would look like, and "how" they'd get paid enough, make that work with kids, or acquire the skills needed. And third, often their stated purpose was their kids; the reason they work so hard and how being a mother was their most important role.

Being a mother is a huge part of an identity, but it doesn't have to be your sole purpose. You can want to solve an important world problem like hunger or climate change, help your teams secure justice or invent new solutions or feel productive, and still do all of that for your children while you're saving the planet. If you have big dreams, you don't have to fit yourself into a smaller box. Maybe your purpose is tied to something outside of work, or to raising good humans and next generation leaders. And if you have no dreams or no time for them or forgot what used to light you up, that's okay too. I'm here to tell you that nobody has it all figured out all of the time; we're all in different states of understanding what feels purposeful to us.

In sum, the hustle culture distracts us from meeting the exact human needs that we are built for. It prevents us from evolving, or simply: from growing. Of course, I must say, not all cultures are toxic and built on hustle culture, not all women feel this way, and not all men want to preserve the status quo. What we're focused on here is examining the impact of hustle culture, and challenging your own mindset and behaviors to see if they need to evolve. Another goal is to spot the cultures that mimic situations that aren't good for you, so you can make informed decisions on what to do next. In the process, you have an opportunity to explore whether there are other models, other ways of looking at work and life, that would allow you and those around you to be fully themselves.

What an Addiction to the Hustle Culture Does to Individuals

When we get caught up in the hustle culture and endlessly chase tasks, we often disconnect from our authentic selves, or give up parts of ourselves in order to belong. The sad result of this disconnect is that, when we live and work in cultures that don't allow us to be fully authentic, we must choose between becoming the person the system will reward, being fully ourselves in a system that will try to change us, or changing the system.

At first, I tried to adopt the behaviors the system would reward. My authentic self actually enjoys peace, being productive, and has a lot of time for other people. But once I tried to race up the corporate ladder *and* have a family, I felt I could never keep up. So, I ran even faster. I was terse with so many around me, particularly when I felt my time was being wasted, and productivity and optimizing my time became more important than what I was actually spending my time on. Efficiency won out over effectiveness which cost me at home, and some deals at work when I didn't spend enough time building a relationship with a would-be client. When we adopt alternate personas or work identities, it costs us our authenticity and peace - we can't speak up when we'd like to and we may even have a different way of speaking and dressing at work versus in 'real life.' Over time, this takes a toll on our souls. As one healthcare executive, Sherry, put it: "When you are not living in alignment with who you are, for an extended period of time, this is what happens. You lose yourself."

While a different angle to this experience, the women of color I interviewed and researched could relate to this concept on a whole different level as microaggressions. These are relatively small comments or moments where racism is at play at work, forcing people of color to constantly think about how to show up so as not to be perceived as one woman called it, "the black angry female." One woman, Tiffany, relayed how working from home showed her just how much of a persona she was adopting to fit into the workplace. Once she stopped having to focus so much on her outfit, keeping her demeanor open and friendly, or whether her hair would be considered professional, she realized she was abandoning herself to fit in. She had lost a whole part of her identity, not just in hustle culture, but because bringing her whole self to work in her workplace would have been deemed "unprofessional." It wasn't safe.

Alternatively, when we stand firm and authentic inside a system bent on making us conform, we are constantly told we are *too much* or *not enough*. The burnout from trying to live authentically inside of a system will show up as character defects or as you being labeled as "difficult." A great example is the difference in how I showed up the year I was being considered for the partnership in my firm (but was ultimately deferred), versus the following year where I reclaimed a bit of my identity, and got promoted. The first year, I had gotten feedback to not speak up too much, but to have an opinion, to be agreeable and "not have sharp elbows" (a term often used about women to remind them to be likable), and to avoid being liked in favor of being respected. Not exactly straightforward advice. That year, I showed up as all the things everyone told me to be, and it showed. I was all over the place. I had no confidence that I was focused on the right things at work and, at home, I was burned out from endless work weeks and two young kids. After I got passed over for the partnership, I regrouped and decided I'd go for it a second time, but only on my terms. I'd limit travel, I'd do what was needed and nothing more, I'd stop caring so much what other partners in charge thought, and decided if they wanted me they'd need to accept me for me. They did, and I was admitted to the partnership. I got so much feedback that year on how much I changed, though it was really more a return to myself. Some call this 'quiet quitting' where you do the job tasks you are paid to do, or give 100% instead of 120%, and stay under the radar in order to preserve your boundaries. My experience with it lasted three years, ending around the time I was promoted to the leadership team which required more travel and longer hours; the hustle culture pace intensified. And I folded on my commitment to play my own game– without even realizing it.

Changing the system itself can be as drastic as a new set of values for corporate America, or can be as incremental as small changes in your current role that impact everyone around you, adding up to collective action. But in thinking about how this applies to the group I'm most interested in, I wondered: if all humans need security, connection, esteem, and purpose, why is the hustle culture so dangerous for *female* executives? My research showed three major reasons: women are at higher risk for burnout, hustle culture reinforces a limiting belief that they're not enough, and because corporate America structurally isn't designed with women in mind.

Higher Risk of Burnout

The hustle culture is so dangerous for women because we are at a higher risk for burnout. The clinical definition of burnout is chronic unmanaged stress, with symptoms across three factors: exhaustion, cynicism, and inefficacy (nothing you do seems to make a difference). It is happening at record levels across genders, but is particularly on the rise for women. Pre-COVID-19, 68% of women reported suffering from burnout, compared to 58% of working men. By 2022, more than 70% of female employees reported experiencing burnout in their jobs, and 62% had taken a day off strictly due to stress.[9] And, at the executive level, 50% of women in the C-suite confirm they are experiencing burnout in their current role.

The increase for burnout in women can be traced to gender imbalances in housework, caregiving, and office work. According to LeanIn.org, women who work full-time and have a partner are putting in 71.2 hours each week on housework and caregiving, while men are spending 51.5 hours per week on those tasks. That adds up to twenty more hours a week for women, or 1,000 hours a year; enough time to be considered a part-time job.[10] But another major culprit is "invisible work" at the office. A report by McKinsey & Co. outlined this trend, showing that only about a quarter of employees say the extra work they're doing is formally recognized (for example, in performance reviews) either "a great deal" or "a substantial amount."[11] The report co-author Marianne Cooper said, "this mission-critical work is in danger of being relegated to 'office housework': necessary tasks and activities that benefit the company but go unrecognized, are underappreciated, and don't

[9] Amanda Schiavo, *Why female employees are burning out at a faster rate than men* (Employee Benefit News, Dec 1 2020).

[10] *Women are maxing out and burning out during COVID-19* (LeanIn.Org and SurveyMonkey May 7, 2020)

[11] *Women in the Workplace 2021* (McKinsey & Co. and Leanin.Org , September 27, 2021)

lead to career advancement."[12] This often becomes the Diversity, Equity, and Inclusion (DEI) and Wellness work, or culture-building work of planning group activities and social events. DEI work has traditionally not counted towards promotions, and even now some companies give lip service to DEI efforts without changing the ways they compensate or promote. The irony: the important work needed to make people feel like they belong, saving companies millions a year in turnover costs, is being taken for granted.

Reinforces the Limiting Belief of Not Enough

Hustle culture hurts women by preying on the feeling that you are not enough. If you feel like you can never catch up and that more always needs to be done, then the concept that you just need to run a *little faster* is a tempting fix. In my coaching practice, feeling as though they're not enough is the number one limiting belief female executives share with me. Even if you aren't acutely aware of the feeling, we have cultural expectations surrounding us and constantly reminding us, from beauty standards to workplace expectations. If you already feel on some level that you need to do more for fear that you're falling behind, and you're in a work or family culture that feeds and rewards that mentality, it becomes as normal as the air you breathe. And you are easy prey.

You may not even notice you're hustling for your own worth, or that you have a *choice*. It's extremely hard to see an alternative where you *are exactly* enough, when you are surrounded by people running to earn more and do more, in order to feel that they are enough. Unfortunately, you are also more at risk of being exploited, used, and manipulated for someone else's agenda.

---

[12] Marianne Cooper, *Research: Women Leaders Took on Even More Invisible Work During the Pandemic* (HBR, October 13, 2021)

In her 2013 book, *Lean In*, Sheryl Sandberg puts the onus for succeeding back on women. Just raise your hand. Just sit at the table. Just *lean in further*. Though Sandberg did say her book didn't address the system, only the women in it– but by then it was too late. In 2014, as I tried to make partner, juggling two elementary schoolers and a two-income household, my boss looked me square in the eye and gave me the feedback of the acceptance committee: "We just have one final question. Are you willing to lean in?" I was floored. *Wasn't I already? How much further could I go?* I suppose he meant I should put work at the top of the priority list, as only 10% of the partners made that year were women, and I was one of them. I saluted and confirmed, and just like that, hustle culture was embedded in my performance review.

But when we are racing, we don't stop to ask if we're running in the right direction, or even if this is what we want. Said one entrepreneur, Paula, of her constant pace, "it felt like the same day over and over, like the movie Groundhog Day." Everyone else is hustling in the same direction, so we just keep going, thinking *this* weekly planner or *that* calendar color-coding system, or downloading these apps, or finishing this project will be the thing that makes your life feel settled.

Structural Faults

Finally, the hustle culture is so dangerous for women because corporate America wasn't designed for them. It was born of the Industrial Revolution and designed for a white male boss with a stay-at-home wife, whose main role was providing for his family monetarily, while the workers produced units of goods. It was not designed for women. It wasn't even designed for men looking for balance, or fathers who want to come home at a reasonable hour and pick up their children from daycare. It was not designed for the move towards a knowledge economy, which happened in the 1990s, which challenges the notion of units of production and moves us towards measuring the impact of our work. It was not designed for wholeness, but instead for productivity, output, and performance. *At any cost.* But we humans are so much more than that. What happens when you try to merge those different aspects of your life– of your identity and your humanity into the current corporate American system? In many work cultures that still reward mostly based on output or using command and control management, it doesn't work. And yet, the culture makes you think YOU are the problem.

 "The two working parents thing just wasn't working for us. We are the living embodiment of trying to figure out a better path, and need to figure this out for the next generation."

When you are addicted to the hustle culture, you must sacrifice parts of yourself to win. You are set up. You must either fail or win at their game at some expense; family, authenticity, purpose, wholeness, innovation, values, identity– you name it. Said another way: you must abandon parts of yourself to fit in. Maybe for you, it's your creative side in favor of producing results. Your warmth that you show at home, but never at work. Your values, like family time or fun. Your ability to be vulnerable. Your time.

I got pulled into the fantasy that climbing the ladder on my terms was achievable, if only I could figure out the right equation to make it work with the system I was navigating. As if I would be the *one* woman in America to finally figure it out. If I could just find the right planner, or a project without travel, or the right childcare support, or build the best team around me. *Then* I could breathe and figure out what fulfills me, alongside the pride I felt in my roles as a mother and rising executive. But I hadn't figured out the long term answer to how to balance all these roles, so I went back to what was familiar...I ran faster to find it. It had to be just around the corner, right?

One year, after returning from maternity leave, I worried about how I was going to keep ascending in my job with this new human who needed me so desperately. One boss suggested that – to stay updated but save time – I should simply read the headlines of *The Wall Street Journal* every day and play my own "game." And for a long time, I tried. But that's part of the challenge. What does playing your own game look like for a woman who has no role models? What about for women of color? Single parents? Women of low-income backgrounds? And, how do you fit that into an existing game already in progress? If the culture is still controlled by output, and there are many willing participants ready to sacrifice other parts of their lives or themselves for performance, how does it ever change? The people at the top of the pyramid will always tell you that they pulled themselves up by their bootstraps and made it happen. Perhaps, more honestly, they abandoned other parts of themselves, and you should too if you want to be financially successful. There's nothing wrong with the system. There must be something wrong with *you*.

What an Addiction to the Hustle Culture Does to Companies

The impact of the hustle culture takes its toll on individual women leaders, but it also hurts the companies it serves. Companies with workplace cultures that embed hustle culture to drive productivity cause three unintended harms. They often put too much focus on profit at the expense of purpose and innovation, stunt the leadership growth of executives, and miss out on key talent.

A Narrow Definition of Success

First, the hustle culture often narrowly defines success as revenue or profit at the expense of purpose and innovation. Sure, capitalism exists to make money and that's what companies do, so it follows that they should be revenue-generating. But, in toxic cultures, there is often a weak strategy or a purpose that is disconnected from profits because revenue IS the only purpose. *Why this obsession with revenue?* On the surface, there is a quarterly shareholder reporting cycle that drives executives to constantly deliver growth. If they don't, they may face the wrath of the market in the form of reduced share price, or the possibility of losing their job.

But if we were to survey the therapists of all C-suites in corporate America, or just apply a little consulting root cause analysis to what is happening in the *minds* of those executives, it might look something like this: 98% of corporate America is run by men. Corporations are measured mostly by revenue because men tie worth to money and security because money and security give them *power*. *Why are they afraid of not having power?* Because, in our society, having power and winning is equated with success; anything else is deemed weak or a failure. So, to win, they've constructed a game with only one way to succeed. In a 2018 survey of venture-backed CEOs on their own mental health, 90% admit that fear of failure is the number one thing keeping them up at night. When asked to name other significant challenges, 49% cited revenue growth and raising capital.[13] It's no surprise the companies they run focus on revenue as king, or increasing share price as the most important goal. For some, this may be an intentional design, but I think the majority have no idea these beliefs are influencing their choices as leaders. That there are other things they could value. That there are other ways to *live*.

---

[13] *2018 Norwest CEO Journey Study.* (Norwest Venture Partners, 2018)

There's been a recent focus on balancing purpose alongside profit, driving new commitments from C-suites across the country. But speaking to your purpose is half the battle; the purpose also needs to be reflected in the actions of its leaders. And that's where culture comes in: how you treat each other. The focus on a "purpose-driven culture" or a balanced scorecard of "well-rounded candidates" falls apart the minute a leader excuses the poor behavior of a jerk who happens to be a sales rainmaker. In toxic cultures or with a toxic leader, there is often a disconnect between what you state externally, and what you tolerate or measure internally. There's an outside image that gets leaders favorable coverage in *The Wall Street Journal*, and then there is the truth and the lived experience that employees or leaders whisper to each other when others aren't listening. One top finance executive quipped, "this job will cost you no less than your blood, and don't be fooled if anyone tells you differently." And, for many organizations, it sets up a disconnect between what they say they stand for and what they reward. As Gruenter and Whitaker wrote, "your culture is only as good as the worst behavior you will tolerate."[14]

 "Your culture is not that great when you watch your mentor have to claw their way to have a voice and be heard."

Innovation can also bring meaning to work, allowing employees to find more purpose and intellectual stimulation in their careers. The overfocus on profit in a quarterly cycle often defunds long-term research and development (R&D) budgets in favor of the product or service that is guaranteed to bring in profitable revenue in a given quarter. Larry Fink, CEO of BlackRock, called out

[14] Steve Gruenert and Todd Whitaker, *School Culture Rewired.* (ASCD, 2015)

the discrepancy in how we measure value in his 2016 letter to fellow CEOs of Fortune 100 companies: "Companies also expose themselves to the pressures of investors focused on maximizing near-term profit at the expense of long-term value."[15]

Not all companies bend to this pressure, however. There are great examples of cultures championing a balance between profit and purpose in the daily experience of their employees. For example, in response to burnout, Microsoft is going beyond tracking employee engagement and measuring the extent to which employees are thriving. Chief People Officer, Kathleen Hogan calls it the Five Ps: pay, perks, people, pride and purpose, and like Maslow's Hierarchy of needs, the levels build upon one another. Microsoft defines thriving as being "energized and empowered to do meaningful work" and actively surveys and measures components across the workforce.

A couple of interesting themes emerged from their studies: managers make a huge impact on the daily employee experience of the company culture, and thriving is not the same as work-life balance, which focuses on time and space to fit other things into your life beyond work.[16] PayPal sought pay equity by making all employees shareholders, and making a targeted increase in net disposable income to help employees manage their overall financial wellness, a metric that it tracks.[17] One CEO in the real estate industry, Linda, shared with me how she not only made her employees shareholders, she limited her executive compensation

[15] Matt Turner, *BlackRock's Larry Fink told CEOs that 'quarterly earnings hysteria' is bad for business — here's the letter he sent them,* (Business Insider, June 14, 2016)
[16] Dawn Klinghoffer and Elizabeth McCune, *Why Microsoft Measures Employee Thriving, Not Engagement* (HBR, June 24, 2022)
[17] Shannen Balogh, *PayPal Workers Were Struggling to Make Ends Meet; CEO Dan Schulman Vowed to Change That,* (SHRM, October 4, 2021)

and turned the excess capital into grants to drive home ownership for low-income renters in the city. That is a strong example of redefining success, and balancing purpose and profit.

Stunts Leadership Growth and Workplace Culture

A rising VP in her 30s, Veronica, shared when she realized the hustle culture would change her if she stayed in her role in a company plagued by burnout. Her male boss had a newborn at home when a deal they were working on blew up; he spent the next 24 hours at the office while his wife struggled alone. The VP thought, "you're an MD in your fifties, and *this* is your life?" Next, she saw her company's solo female leader schedule her C-section so as to not conflict with a client deliverable; she even sent pictures of herself in her hospital gown from her laptop the very next day. Veronica realized this is the behavior being *rewarded,* as modeled by her business unit leaders. That gave her the jolt she needed to plot her career pivot.

Many women I interviewed said they didn't start out as workaholics, but the hustle culture around them made it feel so normal that they adopted the behaviors needed to keep up. Imani, a former consultant, lamented that the language her colleagues used sounded like the military; like a band of brothers on a battlefield, where the leaders could not be questioned. It also made her feel as though she needed to adopt that language in order to fit in, and started to minimize discussion of her private life in favor of the accepted small talk for that male-dominated team: sports, grilling, or weekend plans. I remember this dynamic on one of my teams, and I wound up asking the male associate for a Monday morning summary of all the major sports news that happened over the weekend, well aware that *without this information* I couldn't participate in any of the small talk with clients and colleagues. On the one hand, it helped me fit in. On the other hand, our interactions were reduced to just a single dimension of our lives, excluding people without even realizing it.

Hustle culture attracts leaders who run teams on individualized metrics, and a leadership style of command and control behaviors. This is tied to the hustle mindset of scarcity, and creates a feeling that you are only as good as your last deal. *The impact?* Burned out team members who are unlikely to take risks, as well as understaffing and high turnover. Companies should measure things beyond revenue, but part of the challenge is also in *how* metrics get used to manage performance within the culture. Healthy organizations look at metrics as an indicator of fitness and adjust approaches accordingly, knowing it is about continuous improvement. Toxic cultures are often ruled by the *tyranny of metrics*, as author Jerry Zuller calls it. Metrics are appropriate for diagnosing and analyzing, but "problems arise when such measures become the criteria used to reward and punish."[18]

"Our work culture is not sustainable to have a life. As much as we say we take care of our people, we announced increased mental health support at the same time we introduced utilization increases."

One company I worked with used a 52 metric scorecard to micro-manage its senior leaders. When critiqued on the approach, the leader backtracked and claimed in a company meeting that executives beneath him had misunderstood its purpose. In that case, he could have owned the decision, admitting that publishing a scorecard didn't work as intended, and clarified the purpose of the tool. But that would have required the behaviors of vulnerability,

---

[18] Jerry Z. Muller, *The Tyranny of Metrics*, (Princeton University, 2018).

measuring things beyond profit, and not micromanaging executives. To test whether a company's stated values are lived within
its culture, look at whether the values and purpose are directly
connected to the way the organization makes money, how it is
organized, and how employees and leaders are *incentivized*. Many
interviewees summarized their wish for a different type of leader
or culture to emerge. Donna, an IT executive, explained it as "we
have to create a place where the whole person can come to work."
This goes to the heart of making leadership styles more human.

Key Talent Leaves

When hustle cultures prevail, they weed out the best talent, ham-
pering diversity, innovation, and, often, profitability in the process. Said more simply: their C-suites stay more authoritative,
status quo, white and male. As of 2021, 86% of Fortune 500 CEOs
were white men, while 8% were women.[19] That year, a whopping
five CEOs were non-white.[20] At the board level, the story is slightly
better; 21% of all S&P 500 directors in 2021 were from underrepresented racial and ethnic groups (Black, Asian American, Latinx
or Hispanic, Native American, Alaska Native, or multiracial), and
30% of all S&P 500 directors in 2021 were women.[21] Meanwhile,
research has shown improved performance correlated to diversity, with McKinsey reporting that companies with greater diversity in their leadership teams were 33% more likely to lead their
industries in profitability.[22] And for innovation, companies with
higher levels of diversity generated more income from innova-

---

[19] Dana Wilkie, *How DE&I Evolved in the C-Suite*, (SHRM) and Emma Hinchclife,
The Female CEOs on This Year's Fortune 500 Just Broke Three All-Time Records
(Fortune, June 2, 2021).
[20] David Gura, *You Can Still Count The Number Of Black CEOs On One Hand*, (NPR,
May 27, 2021).
[21] Spencer Stuart. *2021 S&P 500 Board Diversity Snapshot*. (2021).
[22] Vivian Hunt, Delivering through diversity, (McKinsey & Co., Jan 18, 2018, p 1)

tive products over a three-year span than those who did not. The companies with below-average diversity generated 26% of their revenue from innovative products, while those with higher diversity drove 45% of their revenue from their innovation portfolios.[23] Partly to blame is the focus on narrowly defined metrics of success, which then drives individual behavior to do the expected activity that will be rewarded, instead of trying to solve problems differently.

Another driver is that diverse employees are switching jobs at much higher rates than their white counterparts; many citing a lack of diversity at the top. According to the American Staffing Association's poll in late 2021, 64% of Hispanics or Latinos reported they were likely to look for a new job within the next year, compared to 49% of African Americans and 34% of Caucasians.[24] The main reason black employees quit was lack of career advancement; but underneath this statistic lies unequal representation, microaggressions, and treatment at work. Black employees make up just 7% of managers, and one study found that 40% of black women said their qualifications were questioned regularly, while over 80% of BIPOC (black, indigenous, and people of color) women reported experiencing microaggressions at work.[25] While the impacts of the Great Resignation may play out for decades to come, women report having been disproportionately impacted by COVID-19, with 73% of white women and 84% BIPOC women in agreement.[26]

[23] Rocío Lorenzo, *How Diverse Leadership Teams Boost Innovation* (BCG, January 23, 2018)

[24] *Show Them the Money: Pay Is Most Important for Potential Job Seekers,* (Workforce Monitor, American Staffing Association, December 9, 2021)

[25] Savanta, *Black Lives Matter: Everywhere* (Savanta, January 2021).

[26] Alyssa Schaefer, *Survey Finds Great Resignation Continues as Women Seek New Jobs with Higher Income to Compensate for Financial Setbacks Caused by Covid Pandemic* (Laurel Road, Mar 02, 2022)

Some industries haven't seen meaningful shifts for decades, as Helen, a government contracting executive lamented.

 "It's been thirty years, and the industry is just male, pale, and stale."

The problem, in sum: we are feeling humans in a driven world, operating at various levels of awareness. We work in companies led by other humans doing their best, ranging from surviving to thriving. Depending on those executives' own level of awareness, you'll have cultures existing on a spectrum; from healthy ones that encourage humanity and vulnerability alongside profits, to toxic cultures that place profit above all else and sacrifice humanity. Along that continuum are executives in all different stages of rehab from their own addiction to the hustle culture and the underlying tendencies that make it so appealing.

My hope for the future of work is that the more healed executives we get into the C-suite, the more chances we have at getting corporate America to stop hustling for the sake of the hustle, and start leading companies in a way that truly taps into the creative and collective power of their employees. Leading, at a higher level.

CHAPTER 2

HOW WE GET HOOKED

"One of the marvels of the world is the sight of a soul sitting in prison with the key in its hand."

— Rumi

After leaving her job, which she described as *soul-crushing*, digital executive Jackie had made some meaningful changes. She was no longer going to miss her toddler daughter's birthday for work, jump on a plane and fly internationally with no notice, or tolerate 80-hour workweeks. She changed jobs and began to set time boundaries, bracing for the complaints. But Jackie was not prepared for what came next... no complaints! That's when it hit her: "Wait a second– was I doing this all to *myself*?"

As I dug into the makings of the hustle culture, looking for a solution, I wanted to know more about how women got hooked in the first place– and who was responsible. *Do employees and leaders promote this culture without realizing they're stuck in a machine? Are corporations creating this mess by focusing on narrow, one-dimensional metrics? Is it society at-large, which values performance and wealth, telling boys to be tougher and girls to be cuter?* The likely answer? All of the above. After all, a corporation is simply a group of people deciding to act in a consistent or similar way. In fact, the word "corporate" stems from the Latin word "corpus" which means "body."[27] To impact society at large, I believe employees and executives can do their part to understand and take responsibility. Both for their role in their own healing, and in creating a less toxic culture for everyone around them.

When we look at the causes of why women lose touch with themselves on the hamster wheel of the hustle culture, it's clear that there are outside influences– as well as those within us. Macro factors happen outside of you, in your environment, influencing you in certain ways, while micro factors are happening within you and include your beliefs, world views, and even your nervous system. Both produce reactions, some consciously, but many subconsciously. My research and interviews showed that, on a macro level, we are influenced by societal expectations for women, the role of women in the workforce, and the gender imbalances in time related to caregiving.

Macro Factors: Societal Expectations

First, societal expectations for women have largely focused on adhering to socially accepted feminine traits. We can trace this back to Puritan ideals within society, which called for women to be virtuous guardians of the home in order to retain God's favor, leaving the domains of work ethic, earning a living, and voting to men. A woman's most prized role was mother; often described as a helper to her husband. For people who escaped England to find freedom and equality, they may have secured religious rights, but did not disrupt roles and gender norms. Other cultures have mirrored these traditional or patriarchal values, including Latin and Central American cultures, where women were confined to domestic duties and childbearing in the past.

---

[27] Macmillan dictionary blog (2013).

Today, our society still values different qualities in men and women. As of 2015, a poll designed to test these perceptions found that society values physical attractiveness in women as most important at 35%, followed by being empathetic and nurturing at 30%. Female ambition was considered valued by only 9%, and strength by just 5% of respondents. In contrast, for men, society values honesty at 33% and professional/financial success at 23%, with empathy at 11% and being family-oriented at only 5%.[28]

The United Nations argues these stereotypes can be used to justify discrimination against women, but they can also be used to uphold patriarchy, which is simply a society in which men have power, political control, moral authority, and social privilege. In contrast, I love the description of feminism used by the Asian Pacific Institute on Gender Based Violence: "Feminism, which is about women claiming their rights to self-determination and equality, confronts gender conformity and aims to *replace relationships of power with relationships of meaning*." The bottom line: there are expectations about the role you play in society as a woman and where your value is derived from that are at odds with what is expected of you in the workplace.

Macro Factors: Women in the Workforce

The role of women in the workforce is the second macro factor that influences how much hold the hustle culture has, including limitations on the roles that can be played. Female participation in the workforce has changed along with the economy, technological advances, and choices one could make about reproduction. In 1900, female workforce participation was 18%, jumping slightly during World War II, and in the 1960s to 40% around the invention of contraceptive pills, before steadily climbing to

---

[28] Kim Parker et al (Pew Research, Dec 5, 2017).

another plateau at 58% in 2000.[29] As of 2022, 53% of corporate entry-level jobs are held by women, a percentage that drops to 37% for mid-management roles and 26% for vice presidents and senior managers, according to McKinsey & Co.[30] Then came the "mommy wars" of the 1980s and 1990s where women who had these choices suddenly had to *defend* them. Set up as two opposing camps between women who stayed home and those who worked, women defended their decisions, with the outcomes of their children as the proof. They were duped into believing they must fight with each other to retain a moral high ground, instead of realizing they have been marginalized in a workplace, or society as a whole. As author Shannon Drury writes, "the mommy wars, as they stand today, serve as an effective check on the ambitions of the American mother."[31]

And what exactly counts as *work*? Social science research has long documented how characteristics like gender and race shape what gets counted as "real" work and how valuable that work is deemed to be. In the 1980s, sociologist Arlene Kaplan Daniels coined the term "invisible work," describing women's unpaid labor like housework and volunteer work; work that, while crucial, is not really regarded as "work" and is thus culturally and economically devalued or unpaid. Cat, who left the workforce to become a stay-at-home mom, called out this discrepancy in unpaid labor: "Work should either be valued and paid, or it is not valued and is free, but that shouldn't be determined by who

[29] Esteban Ortiz-Ospina, *Sandra Tzvetkova and Max Roser. Women's Employment,* (Our World in Data, March 2018).
[30] Larissa Faw, *Why Millennial Women Are Burning Out At Work By 30* (Forbes, Nov 11, 2011)
[31] Shannon Drury, *The Radical Housewife: Redefining Family Values for the 21st Century.* (Medusa's Muse, 2014).

performs the task." On the job, as mentioned before, "invisible work" often manifests as "office housework."[32]

While women are reaching record levels of burnout, approaching 50% in the executive ranks, this type of overwork isn't new. Corporations, and especially professional services and physicians, have been scrutinized for mental health failings and burnout for decades. In the field of law, it was found 1 in 4 lawyers suffer from psychological distress, including anxiety and depression,[33] and suicide ranks among the leading causes of premature death among lawyers. One lawyer named Amy said, "our profession has lost perspective; we think being a lawyer defines us. That success means being the highest- billing, highest-earning, most productive person there at the expense of taking care of ourselves. That we can't show vulnerability or reach out for help."[34] And it's hurting the companies, too. Burnout and depression takes a financial toll, with the global cost of lost productivity estimated at $1 trillion each year, according to the World Health Organization (WHO).[35]

The systems surrounding these professions are partly to blame, along with a fixed mindset of 'this is how it's always been done' and 'I sacrificed, so you should too.' I witnessed this while my husband was in his surgical residency, just as 100-hour workweek limitations in medical training were being discussed. Some attending physicians who had trained in systems where they worked 100+ hours a week clung to the notion that this

---

[32] Victoria Masterson, *Women are burning out doing invisible 'office housework'* (WEF, Nov 8, 2021).

[33] Benjamin Sells, *"Facing the Facts About Depression in the Profession,"* Florida Bar News, March 1995 and Utah State Bar Journal August/September 2003

[34] Lilah Raptopoulos and James Fontanella-Khan, *The Trillion-dollar Taboo: Why It's Time to Stop Ignoring Mental Health at Work* (FT Magazine, July 10 2019).

[35] *Mental Health in the Workplace*, (WHO, 2016).

was the best training method, despite many studies showing otherwise.

Macro Factors: Imbalances in Caregiving

Third, on a macro level there is a time imbalance in both child and eldercare, mostly along gender lines, leading women to perform a higher proportion of caretaking responsibilities relative to their partners. Unlike every other developed country, the United States has never treated childcare as an essential service. Since at least the 1970s, when President Richard Nixon vetoed a bipartisan effort to implement a universal child care system because it had what he called "family-weakening implications," the industry has been cast as a personal choice — more specifically, a *mother's* choice.[36] Today, the Pew Research Center has found that 74% of mothers say they do more to manage their children's schedules and activities than their spouse, with only 3% saying their husbands do more, while 59% of women say they do more household chores than their spouse, and 6% say their spouse does more.[37] And, in my own experience, Ruth Bader Ginsburg's famous line about the school calling her first still holds true today. No matter how many times I listed my husband first on forms, they always called *me*.

Thinking about the benefits of shifting this dynamic, too little has been studied on the GDP-boosting implications of full female employment that would be helped by childcare. One New York Times article cited the value of unpaid women's labor in the world at $12 trillion, and women's unpaid labor – in the United

---

[36] Alisha Haridasani Gupta, *Child Care in Crisis: Can Biden's Plan Save It?* (NY Times, Oct 6, 2021)
[37] Amanda Barroso, *For American Couples, Gender Gaps in Sharing Household Responsibilities Persist Amid Pandemic* (Pew Research Center, Jan 25, 2021)

States alone – was worth $1.5 trillion.[38] Consider the impact in America if that had been paid labor. What would it do to consumer spending, full employment, and job creation? What could that do to the power imbalance in some homes that benefit the husband, where women don't have the economic power to make choices for themselves and their children?

In addition to these macro constraints contributing to the hustle culture, there are also impacts at a micro level: we hold the hustle culture in place with our mindsets and behaviors. What may be running in the background of your mind and body is a function of several variables: childhood dynamics, the city or town you live in, how you process stress, your values or belief system, and your relationships– to name a few. The impacts of these experiences could get locked into your subconscious like a program running in the background that you're not even fully aware of. You are making decisions in your adult life based on previous events and your reactions to those events, thereby shaping your belief system and influencing your actions.

Micro Factors: Mind

We keep the hustle culture intact on three micro-levels: in our mind, our bodies, and our souls. Beginning with our mind, one of the best quotes comes from the Tibetan philosopher Tsoknyi Rinpoche about our thoughts being "real but not true."[39] We are running on a series of beliefs that formed in reaction to our environment or experiences. Some are healthy – like feeling we are strong and can be anything we want to be – while others are more

---

[38] By Gus Wezerek and Kristen R. Ghodsee, *Women's Unpaid Labor is Worth $10,900,000,000,000,* (NYTimes, March 5, 2020).
[39] Tsoknyi Rinpoche & Swanson, E, *Open Heart, Open Mind: Awakening the Power of Essence Love.* (New York: Harmony Books, 2012).

limiting, feeling we need to prove our worth or being afraid to fail. When the limiting beliefs are in control, we may hold ourselves back from raising our hand in class or from applying for the bigger job until we're confident we'll nail it. These beliefs can impact everything we do; we subconsciously choose careers and romantic partners based on them.[40] As one woman, Camille, quipped to me, "management consulting is for kids of divorced parents" because they grow up accustomed to a parent not always being present.

Someone with a history of abandonment may choose a career where they are needed, like nursing, whereas someone who was taught to downplay emotions may choose to be a doctor or judge, careers where you have to compartmentalize emotions. In corporate America, I noticed a trend of executives who came from a working-class background or parents who immigrated. Later, I recalled these stories and wondered what role they had played in how they prioritized financial security or the drive to prove themselves, above beliefs that may have prioritized purpose or intellectual stimulation.

Micro Factors: Body

Do you ever feel like things are a little too settled or too quiet? Have you ever tried to sit down to read a book, and find yourself jumping back up to put one more thing away before you can let yourself truly relax? Your body and nervous system adjusts to whatever level of activity you feed it. When your nervous system is trained to crave action, you're drawn to activity, stimulation, excitement, and sometimes even instability or a breakneck pace. Even if you know it's not good for you, your body will return to what is familiar. If you've been running hard at work, it's often

---

[40] Dan Neuharth, *Why We Choose the Mates We Do and How to Choose The Best Mate for You,* (Psych Central blog, Aug 14, 2018)

difficult to shift completely into a different pace at home and you end up hustling there too. Some of us keep the pace and activity high because it's all we know. This isn't about what you'd like to do, it's about what your body pulls you towards; just being able to recognize that is an excellent start.

 "When you've been running since you were 16, if you spend 30 years doing that it's really hard to say that's not who you are."

On top of this, women are almost twice as likely as men to be impacted by depression. Though it can hit at any age, depression is correlated to life stages and events, such as puberty, childbirth and menopause, and times when estrogen levels dip. Cultural differences can also contribute to women being more likely to suffer from depression; unequal power and status, workload, and a higher incidence of abuse.[41] One study suggests that the neurotransmitters in women's brains rely primarily on serotonin, a hormone which helps you enjoy life and feel good, while men's brains primarily rely on dopamine, the hormone of competition, risk-taking, and motivation. Addiction specialists surmise that women use up the serotonin in over-nurturing family and friends or excessive worry, and that men deplete their dopamine in over-competition and over-driving themselves. In women, this shows up as depression; in men, as midlife risk taking.[42]

If depression was more prevalent in women, I wanted to examine the historical trend in women's alcohol or substance abuse.

[41] Sandhya Pruthi, M.D. *Depression in Women: Understanding the Gender Gap,* (Mayo Clinic blog).
[42] *The Difference Between the Male and Female Brain,* (The Renewal Point blog, September 2014)

However, I quickly discovered nobody had bothered to measure it. Clinical studies historically only measured the impact of alcohol and drugs on *men*. The National Institutes of Health (NIH) began requiring female participants in studies in 1990; so, the data regarding trends is still relatively recent.[43] But there is a close link between alcohol use and depression, with an estimated one-third of people with major depression also having alcohol/substance abuse issues. *Was this link higher in women?* Yes and no. The differences were attributed to both sex and gender - biological, hormonal and chromosomal differences, and cultural influences such that define how women see themselves, including gender expectations and power imbalances. In biology, women were found to be less susceptible to becoming physically dependent on drugs, such as nicotine or alcohol, but more heavily influenced by social factors and perceptions of holding a cigarette or a glass of wine.[44] So, while some of this dependence on the hustle culture is from your mindset, your biology and own body may also be working against you.

Yet, with newer data, we can see that alcohol dependence in women is on the rise, increasing 83% between 2002 and 2013.[45] In fact, alcohol companies started to shift marketing towards women, in line with consumer trends, and as one study showed, because women are willing to pay 13% more on average to a product that is geared towards their needs. Studies by gender experts have found that women in their 30s and 40s often use alcohol as a means to reclaim - you guessed it - *lost identity*. Researcher Carol Emslie,

---

[43] NIDA, *The Importance of Including Women in Research* (National Institute on Drug Abuse, April 13, 2021)

[44] NIDA. *Summary: Substance Use in Women Research Report,* (National Institute on Drug Abuse, Aug 3 2021).

[45] Irina Gonzales, *Alcohol Marketing is Hitting Women,* ((The Temper, European Centre for Monitoring Alcohol Marketing, Jan 24, 2019).

the leader of the Substance Use research group within the School of Health and Life Sciences at Glasgow Caledonian University in Scotland, found that women drink as a way to reward themselves and draw a line between the work day and home life, to reclaim some of their spontaneity and fun, and "to show their identity beyond what is associated with being a woman in midlife."[46] We've used up all that serotonin in caregiving, we want to belong in a social setting, and sometimes we are using alcohol to reclaim the parts of ourselves that we may have set aside when we pursued building families or careers.

Micro Factors: Soul

Regarding our souls, there are many words across cultures for what happens when we are disconnected from our true selves. It can show up as ignoring our own intuition; a disconnect from our authentic selves; not following God's will in our lives; ignoring that little voice that says 'something isn't right here.' As I began to review some of the decisions I'd made and dream about what I wanted next in my life, I was reminded of these moments where I had ignored something meaningful; I can only describe it now as my soul crying out for a change. I found an old letter from a leadership retreat, where we had to write a letter to ourselves seven years in the future, detailing what our lives looked like and what we had accomplished. At the time I was a young mother, working on a government program, living in the city, and trying to get promoted to the next level of leadership. To do the exercise, a coach was brought in and we were asked to first close our eyes and meditate, imagining we were rising above ourselves– first by a few feet, then above the conference center, before floating all the

<hr>

[46] Mara Altman, *Happy? Sad? Stressed? How Drinking Became the Answer to Everything*, (NY Times, July 6, 2021).

way up into the galaxy. Then, when we'd come back down, it would be seven years from now. We had to try and remember all that we could envision, before coming back to the present and writing the letter to ourselves.

Being a leadership retreat, I was uncomfortable with this new age hypnosis stuff and talk of emotions. I expected to see myself in a corner office or, perhaps, celebrating a career win, surrounded by my family. Instead, the image that came to my mind was me in a horse field in the country with a dog at my feet, hair swept into a ponytail and no makeup, and walking to a farmhouse where my husband, kids and our friends were there for a party. To this day, I can describe the stone fireplace that rose towards the ceiling, the sunflowers on the table, and the feel of the wind on my face. In the letter I wrote, I described a pivot in my life and career towards more purpose, a new product I would launch in a different industry around customer insights and technology, and enriched relationships with my husband and kids. And I'd get there by trusting myself. Reading this letter two months after I had quit, I was shocked. The date of the letter was exactly seven years ago. I had just left my job for more purpose and renewed relationships with my family, and before I left I had built that customer platform that I didn't even have the language to describe seven years prior. The letter my soul wrote to me, telling me I needed to do something drastically different, had been completely forgotten. But it was 100% accurate.

In sum, our environment can hold women back, through formal gender expectations, the role of women in the workforce, and the very real constraints of the 'sandwich generation' of having to care for both children and parents at the same time. The good news: you're not crazy; it's hard to live up to both masculine and feminine ideals at the same time. It is death by a thousand "shoulds." But *you* may be a factor in holding the hustle culture in place, or at least keeping yourself trapped within it. Based on our reactions to what happened to us, we can be more susceptible to becoming addicted. We may be drawn to careers or companies we believe will fulfill the needs we didn't realize we had, or don't know how to fulfill ourselves. But the good news: we can get ourselves out!

So, if both the environment and their own reactions are making some high performing women lose parts of themselves, where does this leave us today? Women who are now in their 40s and 50s are the first generation whose mothers had a choice with their own bodies through birth control, and raised them to be the first generation to choose a career - beyond the three options their mothers had: teacher, nurse, or secretary. We were told we could be anything, so we tried to be *everything*. We are the first generation of women who were raised to 'do it all' but without a guidebook on how, plus shame everywhere for falling short and not doing or being enough.

Ironically, just as we reach a peak upward slope in earning potential, we are often met with very real life choices. Get married, maybe move cities, go to grad school, have a first or second baby. And we do what women tend to do when we make decisions: we look outside ourselves. We talk to friends and look to other leaders in our group, asking for guidance. And we find very few female role models who have both a rewarding career and a fulfilling life, without feeling constant stress.

When women look outside themselves for the answers, three things happen. First, you assume the system is fine and things are working as they should; if you cannot figure out the right mix, that's really *your* fault. You just haven't bought the right planner or downloaded the best scheduling app yet. Second, it is very lonely to try to navigate this on your own with few success stories. How can you decide when to speed up, slow down, go for more, or settle for less when there are no policies, little data, and few examples in your organization? And last, you continue the pattern of relying on someone else to tell you the answer to a question that only YOU can answer.

Once women are given a choice in their own lives, they look around for existing role models…and come up short. Women enter college in higher numbers; as of 2021, women made up more than half of university graduates (53%) but only 8% of CEOs are women;. women of color, just 1%.[47] We make up 56% of front-line employees but only 29% of the C-suite.[48] Women are looking for the elusive model that I'm always asked about; the woman who really does have it all. Every single manager who approached me looking for help and guidance always asked the same thing: "I want a role model who loves her job, loves her family, whose husband works, and who I can respect and admire, and get a glass of wine with. And that's you and one other partner I've heard of. So, how do I create that?" They would perk up when I'd quote the oft-repeated phrase: "You can have it all….just not at the same time and not in the same measure." It gives hope, right? All you have to do is figure out the timing and amount of ambition or nurturing and, like a chemistry experiment, you'll get the balance right. As if life were an equation.

So, why did millions of women leave the workforce in 2020? When the world stopped, and we had a chance to think without distractions, did we look at our work and realize it just doesn't work for us anymore? What brought us meaning in an earlier phase of life no longer makes us feel fulfilled, but we've been scared to let go? Did we look at kids and homes and elderly parents and work

[47] *2021 Women CEOs in America Report*, (Women Business Collaborative (WBC) with Ascend, C200 and Catalyst, 2021).
[48] Gartner 2021 Leadership Progression and Diversity Survey, which queried 3,500 employees across 24 industries on the topic in February 2021.

schedules and say, something's gotta give? Or did we finally realize that the current game is stacked against us?

 "The Great Resignation wasn't about people ditching their jobs; it was about people being ruthlessly honest with themselves about what they want."

In the words of one partner I spoke with, "the older women get, the lower our tolerance for bullshit. Men reach a career pinnacle and tend to say 'yay, I'm in charge!' We reach the same place and say 'this is it?'" And often, we find that reaching a career pinnacle is not the crescendo of our identities, or of the value we bring to the world. There's a lot more. If we have the courage to ask the *right* questions.

CHAPTER 3

THE MAKING OF IDENTITY

"Find out who you are and do it on purpose."

- Dolly Parton

With two toddlers and another two babies in rapid succession, Amy, a retail executive in Manhattan, first cut out hobbies in order to make time for her growing family. But when her job was redefined and her role cut back, she decided the tradeoff was no longer worth it. There was no way she would ever find a career that would give her the fulfillment she wanted with the flexibility she absolutely needed. "So I just let that part of myself go," Amy said. "And, in doing that, I lost a huge piece of myself without even realizing it." Letting go of her ambition and work identity gave her space for other priorities when her kids were small, but she hadn't realized that the drive to create and lead and contribute outside of the home was still a very real part of her.

I believe women have lost themselves. We lose ourselves both daily, and slowly over time, crushed slowly by the weight of the roles we play, and stuck in the hustle culture. Constantly on the go, filling our plates with more things, and trying to be everything to everyone else. Feeling that some part of us is bad or not enough, or believing someone else's version of what our lives should look like. Sometimes, we fake it till we make it. Instead of getting in touch with who we are and understanding our unique gifts, realizing if we tapped into them we'd be infinitely more impactful. It's pretty much the plot of every Disney movie; tap into your inner Elsa to let it go and stop trying to hide your gifts, Moana to remember who you are, and Jasmine or Ariel to find your voice and ask for what you want.

I get it. I lost myself too. First, around seven years old when I began to learn how the world wanted me to act. I felt too much, was too sensitive, and didn't push myself as much to hustle– to achieve. So, I changed. I threw myself into sports and school and leadership positions, and watched as I got validation and medals and approval. Once I learned to hide the parts of myself that seemed too vulnerable, too needy, too much, and started to perform and achieve, I got praise. My impressionable child mind figured out *that's* how you get love and acceptance. An overachiever was born.

I lost myself again in a teenage relationship; making myself small to understand how to fit in *his* needs. Then, again in organized religion, believing all they told me about what a woman should be. Again, in motherhood as this newfound identity was a role I had to now fit into an overachiever lifestyle. And, finally, in corporate America, where I was told to soften sharp elbows, not speak up too much, and, in return, received more validation from colleagues and clients on my 60+ hours a week performance. But losing ourselves assumes we knew who we were in the first place; I'm not convinced many of us actually do.

"It's like I have two lives; my work life which is easier, and then raising teenagers. I think I lost a decade and didn't even know who I was anymore, and am only now filling back in parts of my identity."

A woman's worth has long been defined by the value she provides to others as opposed to having inalienable rights of her own. From the founding of the country, Abigail Adams wrote to her husband John, as they were forging the Constitution, to "remember the ladies" or else "we will not hold ourselves bound by any laws in which we have no voice or representation." And, 200 years later, I'm not certain how well that is working out for us. Traditionally "feminine" ideals for women to be subservient to men have been explained via Biblical verse, biology, and even – incorrectly – by brain size.

Though now refuted in science, in 1895, social psychologist Gustave Le Bon used a portable cephalometer to run experiments and assert that women "represent the most inferior forms of human evolution" based on the diameter of their heads alone.[49] But the role of second-class citizen (and that is only if she was white) and the ideals of what it meant to be feminine were reinforced via popular culture: the Puritan role of a woman to love, obey, and further her husband's will, Victorian ideals of purity and modesty, slavery and the myth of the genteel plantation wife, magazine ads through the 1950s portraying a housewife delivering a martini to a working husband, and the roles women should take in the workplace. In each case: letting someone else tell you what a "good" wife/mother/woman looks like, conveniently defined by the men who benefited from her fulfilling those ideals. Her virtue was in serving everyone else.

As women, we are also conditioned to think our identities are a composite of the roles we play. We are in the middle of a Venn diagram, balancing roles of wife, mother, daughter, sister, worker, friend– and, somehow, we're supposed to balance the needs of

---

[49] Lise Eliot, *Neurosexism: the myth that men and women have different brains* (Nature magazine, March 6, 2019)

ourselves. *Guess who loses that game?* Looking back, I can see how we lose ourselves in big moments of stress or role shifts in our lives; motherhood, marriage, a really stressful job or promotion, disease, caring for aging parents or spouses. When my dad was diagnosed with prostate cancer, my mom joined a support group and they mentioned therapy. She assumed they meant for him; but it was for the wives. They had become full-time caregivers and attended all the doctors appointments, and could easily feel that they were yet again giving all of themselves away in this new role that they never wanted but found themselves in. When I had my babies, I remember feeling like maternity leave was simultaneously the simplest and hardest thing I had ever done. All I had to do was focus on one thing: keeping my newborn fed and alive. It was equal parts beautiful and rewarding, mixed with mind-numbing and depleting.

"You can start to lose yourself in all the roles you play, and those roles become verbs: I mother, I daughter, I work."

To complicate matters, many of us are stuck in a survival or scarcity mentality that runs in the background of our subconscious, feeding us limiting beliefs and keeping us from truly knowing ourselves. When we are stuck in survival mode, we tend to believe the world is out to get us (and sometimes it is) but this mentality can stick with us, embedded like a well-worn path inside our brains. The alternative is to approach the world with an abundance mentality, or a growth mindset. Staying in survival mode can make you apprehensive to change, hyper-vigilant for the next bad thing to happen - whether that's the kids getting sick (again) or worries about a job or getting cancer. We're constantly triggering our fight or flight response, losing ourselves and our connection to ourselves in the process.

What does it look like to lose ourselves in real life?

- It shows up as not feeling enough; not *doing* enough, not *giving* enough, not *having* enough. So, instead, you keep a fully packed calendar of all the things, crossing things off lists until you feel like you've done 'enough.' You choose a job or a partner who hustles so you can provide enough for yourselves and your children.

- It shows up as looking outside of yourself for confirmation of the things that only you can possibly know. As Glennon Doyle so beautifully states in her book *Untamed*, of women who finally realized this, "we stopped asking directions to places they've never been."[50] That book was a key first step in me slowly realizing how trapped I had become. I found I was in a high-powered job, managing 200 people and a multi-million dollar business unit and effortlessly making big decisions at work and, yet, at home constantly asking my husband for his opinion on the smallest things. *Which route would likely have less traffic? What type of coffee should I get?* He doesn't even drink coffee. *Why did I think I needed his input on something he knows nothing about?* Or the big questions, like was this job really what I'm meant to do with my life?

- It shows up as over-identifying with the roles we play. Feeling that your worth as a human comes from those roles, instead of being fully worthy just for being born. Let that sink in. You've seen the mom who has to post on Instagram or Facebook every single thing she does, as if she needs to prove to herself and everyone else that she's living her best life. You may have seen the executive who feels self-important

---

[50] Glennon Doyle, *Untamed*. (The Dial Press, 2020).

because people respect him or her at work. They don't have much else to talk about if not the job, and they'll gravitate back to it when conversations lag. I was probably both of those people.

Inside, I was dying under the weight of trying to perform all the roles at the same time. It took me burning everything down to realize this: you can't be everything to everyone. Not without some conscious choices and tradeoffs. American society and corporate structures aren't set up for you to be fully human as a female executive. They actually need you to perform your roles. Be the mom so your husband can be the executive. Be the worker who is a good corporate soldier churning out profit without asking too many questions about the strategy or seeking balance. That works suspiciously well for men in this scenario. But it doesn't always work for women. As Sarah, a high-powered executive in banking put it, "everyone who was in a position of power either had no kids or someone at home who was taking care of the kids. In my case, as a single mom, the travel requirements of the job were not compatible with my life." The system was, quite simply, not intended for her.

If we're going to find out who we are and *do it on purpose* as Dolly Parton reminds us, including what role your work identity takes, first we need to ask these questions: *what is identity made of? How does your tendency to lose yourself show up differently depending on your stage of life? What role do underlying motivations and beliefs have, based on the generation into which you were born? What about race, gender, and sexuality?*

The Making of Identity

The concept of identity is the perception of ourselves or sense of self, and includes attributes like values, purpose, experiences, and relationships to help describe the things that make up your self image. Psychologist Erik Erikson pointed out that identity evolves over time, by aligning to stages in the human lifecycle. For example, during adolescence, there is often a conflict between identity and role confusion; who you are versus the role you take in your family, or what you feel and believe. Major events and new roles often prompt similar questions, such as becoming a new parent.[51] Some of the key elements that can influence your sense of self include your degree of individuation and having a sense of self, the types of attachments you formed as a child, and the degree of acceptance you experienced, or how likely you are to be authentic versus adopt a persona around certain people in order to be accepted.[52] One lightbulb moment for me was understanding the difference between self-confidence, or belief in your abilities, and self-esteem, or your overall evaluation of yourself. For me, it explained why I had always felt both confident and doubtful, which was confusing. I have typically been mega-confident walking into a room to present my work because I'm certain of my networking and presentation abilities. But I used to be much more uncertain when it came to how I felt about myself or how confidently I shared an opinion. Said another way: I was certain of my ability to perform, but a little unsure of whether the rest of me was enough.

Life Stages

From my interviews, the most obvious changes in identity clustered around changes in the stages of life. Many of the women I interviewed discussed identity impacts when they had babies; or more precisely as they were raising toddlers. Several described this

[51] Tija Ragelienė, *Links of Adolescents Identity Development and Relationship with Peers* (Journal of Canadian Adolescent and Child Psychology, March 2016).
[52] Alex Klein, *"Who Am I?' How to Find Your Sense of Self* (Healthline blog, June 2020)

phase in their lives as a time where they realized that they needed more in their identities and lives, and raising small children was physically taxing. "I felt disconnected, like nothing mattered," recalled one entrepreneur, Beth. Lily, a communications executive, shared that she needed more for herself outside of being a mother and putting her career in the slow lane to accommodate kids. When she had the opportunity to take on more responsibility and mental challenge, she leapt at the chance and loved it, though it came with the tradeoff of 30% more travel. Still, she said, "I felt like I was finally getting to see the me who had been asleep for some time." These were all women who deeply loved their children, but whispered to me confessions that they had other parts of themselves they didn't want to lose.

Another group emerged in the women over 50, who made bold moves in this stage of life to reconnect with themselves. Some worked all the way through and, as they approached 50, some lost parents and friends and realized they wanted to use their time differently in this phase of life. For some, this message was delivered via a health scare, like Sarah who had an emergency quadruple bypass surgery and was forced to scale back her work, but took that newfound time to get involved in a heart-related charity as part of her recovery. Others exited the workforce with transferable skills in their early 30s, stayed home for ten years, and went back once their kids were in high school, founding their own companies or reinventing their careers.

Kate, a finance executive, left a high-powered job after her second child was born, opened her own venture firm when the kids were slightly older, and was thrilled that she's now making more on her own terms than she would have had she stayed. Mary went back to work as a lobbyist after taking off seven years to be home with her children, but kept the relationships active and did contract work along the way so that her transition back to the workforce would be smooth. For some, money was a concern throughout; for others, they were more financially successful in their second act, and more confident running their lives on their own terms.

Generational Impacts

Although the life stage that women are in could be a factor, generational attitudes towards life and work can also be at play. Several studies have been done about how generations are influenced by the larger socio-cultural environment of the time periods into which they were born. Fewer studies, however, cover the values, goals, and relationship to community, which gets into the heart of identity. One study on generational differences in young adults was conducted over forty years and showed some interesting results. At the time of the study's conclusion in 2009, Millennials and GenX'ers rated being very well-off financially, being a leader in the community, living close to parents and relatives, and having administrative responsibility for the work of others as more important than Boomers did at the same age. But these comparisons were also relative. Although the importance of "finding meaning and purpose in my life" decreased and "having lots of money" increased with younger generations, Millennials still rate finding meaning and purpose as more important than having an abundance of money.[53] In this case, the study showed that, even when they hit the life stage of needing to support a family, the priority of finding meaning and purpose was still most important.

Past studies showed that Boomers in America, born between 1946-1964, were a generation shaped by war and fear, with a sense that the world is a scary place. This is especially the case for the earliest Boomers. This was somewhat tempered by post-war optimism, a

---

[53] Gentile, Campbell, & Twenge, 2012; Stewart & Healy, 1989; Twenge, 2006

landing on the moon and space race, and a rebirth of the American dream with a white picket fence, kids and a dog as the antithesis to the horrors of war. There was a tendency to "not air dirty laundry" or talk about "skeletons in the closet," which could be attributed to 1950s McCarthyism and conformity, parents who had seen the horrors of war and were trying to encourage their children to focus on the positives in life, or attitudes towards mental illness during those decades. Their attitudes towards work are generally attributed to the stability that a good job brings, and loyalty in a role being rewarded by tenure. Some of the younger Boomers were more impacted by the self-help movement of the 1960s, which earned them the nickname the "Me Generation" and then devolved into the selfishness and narcissism associated with the 1980s.[54]

Generation X was born between 1965 and 1980. Their cultural influences were the rise of MTV, a rise in divorce or single-parent homes, and Boomer parents who prioritized financial security. They are the first generation of women told they can be anything, with higher college attendance rates, but delayed having children and had higher rates of divorce. Their attitude towards work is to identify with a job and stay somewhere once they've made a decision, trying to make it work.

Millennials or Gen Y were born between 1981 and 1996. The older part of this cohort saw the emerging digital world as a place to share emotions during adolescence, often termed "digital pioneers." Millennial women are burning out at record rates, and asking themselves the question: *How do you prevent getting addicted or losing your identity in work in the first place?* A 2020 Harris survey with Meredith found that 74% of Gen Z women stated "after watching my parent(s) burn themselves out

[54] Tom Wolfe, *The Me Decade and the Third Great Awakening* (NY York Magazine, Aug 23, 1976).

at work, I am making an active effort to find more balance in my life." Millennials don't just work for a paycheck; they want to work for organizations with a mission and purpose.[55] At the same time, many saw their parents impacted by recession and, in response, they value financial security.

The most recent addition to the workforce is Gen Z, born between 1997 and 2012. They are digital natives, and also the most diverse generation; researchers predict Gen Z will be the last generation that will be predominantly white.[56] Watching parents take huge financial hits during the 2009 Great Recession, many Gen Zers are also driven by pragmatism and security, valuing stable jobs and smart investments. They are shrewd consumers, politically more progressive compared to previous generations, and talk more openly about anxiety, depression, and therapy.

And the next generation, back to Generation Alpha or Gen A, starts with children born in 2012 and will continue at least through 2025. Researchers now have this cohort in mind as they look to predict trends, rethink the education system, and reimagine the world of work.

"There's a generational difference in attitudes towards work; Baby Boomers feel indebted to the firm, Gen X'ers are still chasing that corner office; Millennials are financially concerned, but Gen Z is not here to work their lives away."

---

[55] *How Millennials Want to Work and Live* (Gallup Report 2021)
[56] *The Changing Child Population of the United States Report* (The Annie Casey Foundation, January 2011).

Personal Identity: Race, Gender, and Sexuality

Beyond generational cohorts, how you self-identify and the messages or treatment you receive from others can vary along the lines of race, gender and sexuality, and the intersectionality of traits. This is particularly impactful if you belong to a marginalized group, such as women of color, LGBTQ, differently abled, immigrants, or neurodiverse individuals. People whose identity includes anything not accepted as "mainstream" could have even more challenges in losing themselves. You could struggle with the internalized pain or shame of wanting to be accepted. Externally, you could be treated differently for it. Marginalized groups statistically deal with more trauma, pay inequity, and experience slower rates of promotion relative to members of non-marginalized groups.

For gender, it's important we understand what we mean biologically as compared to expectations of roles. Dr. Amanda Solomon Amorao shares that we live in a "...system of gendered relations and ideologies in a specific culture in a specific historical period that dictates what it means to be a man or woman."[57] In her book, *Quit Like a Woman*, author Holly Whitaker outlines why male advice often didn't work for her– from getting promoted to quitting drinking. Often, the solution was to humble herself and explore her own shortcomings. Whitaker believes those of us who already feel shame will be harmed by those asking us to be even smaller. I recall asking one boss for feedback when I felt like I wasn't keeping up, and he said, "If I constantly tell you how good your work is, your head won't fit through the door." Little did he know I seemed to have the opposite problem: not believing in myself enough.

And a note about the men. The limiting beliefs, the position of women in the workplace, the patriarchal systems that run in

[57] Lena Schmidt, *How To Find The Balance Between Your Masculine & Feminine Energy*, (Chopra blog, May 2019)

the background are all _real_ impacts to women's leadership. My interviews and research showed me women want more from their lives. *But so do men.* The approach to rehab and the call to action includes everyone. I interviewed and researched to see how these trends change by gender, and found that men need to be heard, seen, and validated too. But the challenges they face are different. The limiting beliefs, advancement in the workplace, conditioning by society, all leave them in a very different place. I found it impossible to cover both adequately without dramatically weakening the impact and weight of the women's stories I was entrusted with.

You should be able to define what you want and chase it. And nobody can define what that is except you. But you need to be able to identify your needs, wants, dreams, unique gifts, and values, and figure out how to get those needs met and dreams achieved in a *healthy* way. At the same time, there are serious structures standing in the way of achieving this; racism and imbalances of power and opportunity, sexism and imbalances of expectations and roles, capitalism and the imbalance of power in financial structures.

Many of us are struggling and truly just surviving; many don't have the benefit of privilege to stop and ask what it is we really want. Many of us are black and brown and have stories and lenses to add on top of the experience described above. Many of us don't want children or marriage, and don't feel our own life ambitions are seriously considered or accepted. But if you're dying under the weight of your roles...read on. It's not your fault. But it *is* your responsibility to change it.

Identity is made up of so many parts, it's no wonder it's necessary to reconnect with every part in order to build the next chapter of your life with great intention.

---CHAPTER 4---

WHY DO WE NEED REHAB?

"You're your problem, Annie. And you're also your solution."

— Melissa McCarthy, Bridesmaids

A t first, she simply couldn't see well. Small dots flashed before her eyes. But pretty quickly, somewhere above 10,000 feet, she lost the ability to speak. That's when Leigh knew she was in trouble. A consultant in her 30s, she had hopped her usual weekly flight from Florida to Texas, and opened her laptop to work on the plane. But suddenly, Leigh couldn't see very well. She tried to power through, but when the flight attendant asked if she wanted a snack or drink, she spoke in complete gibberish. Back on the ground, she was diagnosed with exhaustion due to stress; she knew something had to shift. She ditched her city life, moved to the mountains, and never looked back.

So, why do we need rehab from the hustle culture? Quite simply: we weren't designed for this. Working at this pace, going so long without rest, having digital interactions instead of physical ones. The pace of the hustle culture makes us think that we have operated at this level for so long, that we often believe we have cheated the system. I'm the one woman in America who will manage to fit 25 hours into a day. Ask any mom of a newborn; she is shocked at how well she adapts to functioning on just four hours of sleep. When asked how they cope, several women I spoke with said, "I just didn't sleep much." The nature of this addiction – both to the pace of the hustle culture and the elements it glorifies – is that we're duped into thinking we are the problem.

As a result, women's levels of depression, anxiety, burnout, heart disease, and loneliness are off the charts. We are hurting. And this addiction to the hustle culture takes its toll on our minds, our bodies, and our spirits.

Mind

One of the most profound things I discovered throughout my own corporate rehab was this mindfulness quote from Tsoknyi Rinpoche: "Our thoughts are real, but they may not be true." This concept literally blew my mind. Beliefs I had come to think were just "the way things are," might not actually be true. These "limiting beliefs" can hold you back from doing things that may otherwise help you grow. Most often in my coaching practice I hear beliefs like, *there's not enough time/clients/money, I need to hurry*, and *I need to constantly prove myself*. I cringe thinking of all the decisions I made from this place rooted in both confidence and fear.

Body

Your body can literally trap and store stress in your tissues, leaving your nervous system dysregulated and craving the type of environment it has adjusted to, often a dysfunctional one. As I interviewed women for the book, I noticed that many of them had experienced a physical manifestation of the stress their bodies were under. Jane, a mom and retail executive, recalled throwing up each morning— but only on weekdays. She attributed it to stress. When I asked

Jane how long this went on for, she paused before wondering to herself, "about 18 months, I think?" *She threw up five days a week for a year and a half.*

Ruth, an executive in her mid 50s, recalled being rushed to the emergency room for what she thought was a heart attack. Doctors ran a series of tests only to find nothing wrong with her heart. Instead, she was suffering from *chronic unmanaged stress.* Lauren, another woman I interviewed, began losing her hair and was diagnosed with an autoimmune disease while holding down two jobs and raising three toddlers. Several women had developed cancer, and I couldn't help but think of the symbolism: after years of being pushed beyond their limits, their bodies were attacking themselves at a cellular level.

Statistics back this up, with surveys showing women are more stressed than men, citing trouble sleeping, poor management of their health, and financial stress. The major causes included heavier workloads at work and at home, gender discrimination, and pay inequity. In fact, one Columbia University study found a link between executive women's gender pay gaps and higher rates of anxiety and depression, and no link between these where a pay gap did not exist.[58]

As for the impacts on our bodies, much has been studied on how the "body keeps the score," as author Bessel van der Kolk writes. Stress, trauma, and abuse can get stored within our bodies and internalized, often showing up in the region of the body that was subjected to it. He tells stories of children who experienced physical or sexual abuse who later develop diseases in those parts of the

---

[58] Katherine Keyes, *Wage Gap May Help Explain Why More Women Are Anxious and Depressed Than Men,* (Columbia University, 2016)

body, and adults who cannot explain their unhealthy behaviors until they process stored memories that have been blocked away.

Spirit

Rise and grind. Soul-crushing. This job is killing me. We hear these phrases played out in pop culture or memes as they relate to the disconnection we feel from our purpose when we work jobs that aren't meant for us. When we live in a survival state, it kills our purpose and connection and keeps us running on fumes. We're more likely to be drawn to unhealthy coping mechanisms, like the hustle culture, and we assign more meaning to the place work occupies in our lives.

So, *why heal?* Because not dealing with your stress or lack of fulfillment or overwork keeps you running on a system of thoughts that may not be true, storing the toxins and stress in your muscles and cells, and damaging your soul. *Who wants that?* After years of therapy and a recent divorce, one woman named Beth discovered, "we repeat what we don't repair."

How I Approached Healing

When I first left my job and was trying to decide what to do next, trapped in my house in the middle of a raging pandemic, I threw myself into my own recovery. I knew I was burned out. But I had no idea where to start. In between getting the kids settled into their online school platforms, I began to read and watch everything I could get my hands on regarding psychology, leadership, neuroscience, and healing. I began therapy for the first time. I started journaling and began taking notes, cataloging all the concepts I was learning. I'd go on walks with friends or answer women's frantic DMs or texts asking for help, teaching them what I'd learned so they could navigate these decisions for themselves. I quickly realized I needed something I could easily pass on. Sending a female entrepreneur or working mother the library of recommended books, videos, articles, and podcasts would be *completely* overwhelming.

I began by looking at standard recovery principles. By no means am I equating hustle culture with substance abuse, but the parallels in paths to recovery are similar. In researching the steps for Alcoholics Anonymous, I was shocked by how much they mirrored the process I was putting myself through; detaching from old mindsets and behaviors that were no longer helping but actively hurting me.

Simplified Recovery Process[59]*:*

- Admit we have a problem; that our lives have become unmanageable.
- Believe that we have a greater power to restore us to sanity, and decide to no longer rely on ourselves and old ways of being.
- Make a fearless moral inventory of ourselves, admit our wrongs, and be ready to remove our defects and shortcomings.
- Make amends.
- Improve our consciousness to understand our deeper purpose.
- Live our lives this way and tell everyone we know.

Next, I focused on learning more about neuroscience, physiology, leadership, workplace wellness, psychoanalysis, meditation, spirituality, religion, and wellbeing. Across practices, formats, cultures, and time, I noticed that certain themes kept repeating.

---

[59] *There are several official steps in multiple recovery processes; some refer to God's will. To make this broadly understandable and applicable, I've simplified the steps, making you the main character in your own recovery.*

Key Themes:

- *Scarcity vs. Abundance Mindset*: The perspective that the world and its resources are scarce, and someone getting more of one thing means you will get less of it. This may be the grandfather to the hustle culture; it breeds a mentality of getting in line first, hoarding finances or things, saving or spending past the point of what is needed, and an "us vs. them" theme popping up in a lot of your conversations. If you don't get yours, you'll miss out. The opposite is an abundance mindset where there is enough for everyone. You can take what you need without hoarding resources. How you behaved in the great toilet paper shortage of 2020 may be a good indicator of which mindset you tend to adopt.

- *Being Enough*: The belief that you need to prove your worth via performance, wealth accumulation, or other extrinsic motivators, rather than understanding the worth that comes simply from being born and being here. Not usually a conscious thought, it often shows up disguised as something else; I need to get more done (not fast enough), I should be more attentive to the kids (not a good enough mother), I need to get back in shape (not thin enough), etc. Could be born out of a scarcity mindset.

- *Fixed vs. Growth Mindset*: This concept is based on whether your abilities are natural and fixed at birth such as talents or gifts, or whether they can be built and nurtured. You may not be great at a new skill... *yet*.

- *Neuroplasticity*: The mind is malleable, and you can rewire past subconscious or conscious thoughts and patterns by replacing old beliefs with new ones. If you have learned to do things, you can also learn to *undo* them.

- *Inner Child*: While we're discussing selves, it's worth noting that psychologists will often refer to an *inner child*, or a younger version within you with beliefs or wounds based on your experiences. This inner child is trapped in the mature version of you now, and you may act out from that younger wounded place at times.

- *Future Self*: In contrast, this is the future version of you; a healed, whole, peaceful version that you may be looking to become in the future, and can be used to anchor choices you are making in the present.[60]

So if we have lost ourselves, and get addicted to the hustle culture to cope, then how do we break this addiction? And how do we start to heal?

We can go to Corporate REHAB.

Like any addiction, we can go to rehab. I created a methodology called the Corporate Rehab leadership framework© that is based on my own experiences, the stories of 300 executive women, and backed by the research from neuroscience to psychology, to take you through a process to do your own rehab from the hustle culture:

Corporate REHAB leadership framework:

- Recognize your life's story
- Evaluate your patterns and relationships
- Heal your mind, body and spirit
- Arise and reconnect with yourself
- Build new dimensions of your career and life

---

[60] Nicole LePera. *How to Do the Work*. (Orion Spring, 2021).

Recognize your life's story

Imagine a vision for the future, and explore the context of your past: your life story, values, beliefs and choices.

Evaluate your patterns and relationships

Evaluate and examine how stress and trauma impact your brain, body and energy - and how that influences limiting beliefs, your nervous system and hormones, and your energy and relationships. This phase is about understanding what mentality keeps us trapped in survival mode, so that we can shift into thriving.

Heal your mind, body and spirit

Nurturing the mind, body and spirit, by letting go of old beliefs, adopting new behaviors, and focusing on your areas of strength.

Arise and reconnect with yourself

Reconnect with the authentic parts of you in three parts: know yourself, grow yourself into new ways of being by building new patterns, behaviors and play, and show yourself by stepping into your strengths and showing up authentically.

Build new dimensions of your career and life

Declare your vision and purpose, gather your crew for support, and chart a course for the career and life you intentionally want to live.

The following chapters outline each section of the Corporate Rehab leadership framework©, walking you through other women's stories, concepts to master, and a series of tools to assist you on your own journey.

I began running women through the Corporate Rehab program, and gathering the stories of all those who had quit the hustle culture, and what they had learned. Many were looking to reset their relationship with their career, others working up the nerve to leave a toxic workplace, and still others focused on leading without burning out. Some wouldn't change a thing because they believed they were finally financially stable enough to have options. Shani, a lawyer, was clear in her advice: "You need to accelerate because you have more agency and can delegate, and *then* slow down; don't try to slow down and then accelerate later. That path and re-entry is too hard...though maybe it shouldn't be." Others wished they had made conscious choices sooner. Veronica would have launched her own businesses earlier, if she could have gotten connected to a potential co-founder and understood the fundamentals of being an entrepreneur. Aniyah would have trusted her instincts, telling me, "what your body and your mind are telling you loudly is worth listening to; everything else is just noise."

Let me be clear about my intentions in helping you do this work. **This process is not about *quitting your job*.** It's not even about leaving corporate America. It's about ditching the hustle culture and leading from a really authentic place so that YOU are the one who decides whether that's from a corner office or a corner of your house. I believe so strongly in doing this work because we need more women in places of leadership. We need your ambition. We need your ideas. We need your style of collaboration. But we also need you to be whole. And that means learning how to lead without losing yourself in the process.

---CHAPTER 5---

RECOGNIZE: OWNING YOUR STORY

*"I have great respect for the past. If you don't know
where you've come from, you don't know
where you're going."*

— Maya Angelou

I wasn't an all-out workaholic... *at first*. I just found more parts of my identity wrapped up in the job, taking for granted that I'd always be a wife and mom; the mundane tasks of cooking and cleaning and carpooling could be done by someone else (yay outsourcing!), while I saved my brain for things that really required it. I got a *lot* done in a typical day, achieving 120% of my tasks, yet still disappointed I couldn't hit 150%. I didn't know it at the time but I was suffering from *Superhero Syndrome*, or the less flattering "time arrogance" where you think you can get more done than the average person. I probably thought that because I was, as most mothers today in America, held to a higher standard than fathers. On the job, those multitasking skills came in handy. But the pace just wasn't sustainable.

In the process, I put myself and my own needs last. It's super dangerous, yet it's what women and moms are conditioned to do. It was really the perfect consultant mindset– just applied to life.

Go through all the tasks and activities, determine where the talent lies or what your differentiator is, and outsource the rest: the mundane, the commoditized, the non-value-added activities. And, in many ways, it worked! I was at every school event, and all the corporate pitches; I tried to operate as both a full-time worker and a full-time mother. In an anecdote (that now makes me cringe), I once hosted a partner breakfast in the morning in Virginia, raced home to DC to change and volunteer at field day for the kids school in a T-shirt, then sped home to pick up a suitcase and fly to NYC in time to host another black tie dinner that night. I'm exhausted now just thinking about it.

But in all my process and time efficiency, I didn't realize a big detail. **You can't optimize emotions. Or connection**. You can't outsource or choose the times when a friend will be mean in second grade. You can't control when your kindergartner will really miss you on that overnight trip. And I didn't really acknowledge what kept me trapped on the hustle culture treadmill in the first place. I didn't fully realize any of this until I stepped off.

When I left my corporate job after twenty years in the industry, I knew I had made the right move for me. I was burned out; underinvesting in my husband, children and myself, on planes three days a week — and it was still never enough. There was always the next hoop to jump through (and, yes, a circus metaphor is totally fitting). But what I didn't expect is how many seemingly happy colleagues around me were secretly miserable - and wished they could be making the same choice.

I was on an upward trajectory, leading a business unit, being primed for several other leadership positions, and (mostly) well-liked and respected by my fellow partners and teams. I had made a name for myself and built a personal brand around being insightful, always on and willing to help, a hard worker and leader with very high expectations, but also kind and interested in the personal lives of my colleagues.

As I submitted my resignation and word got out, the calls and texts began pouring in. From the senior female partner who texted, "I just heard an awful rumor - tell me it's not true," to my peers who called saying, "I heard you resigned and that can't be - you were the one who had it all figured out...what do you know that I don't?," and the twenty-somethings who worked on my team who said, "You can't leave! You're one of the most human partners we have here." I took every call. I wanted to explain myself and share my newfound wisdom. Maybe I could help others - if they only realized what I now knew: they had a choice all along.

As a true people pleaser, I had always prioritized other people's time, and as a leader you're often putting out fires. But by the final month before I quit I started to notice my calendar was full of 12 hours of meetings and calls to deal with *other* people's problems. My exit was no different. I talked to 75 people on the way out; 20 clients, 15 team members and about 40 partners, including a handful of executives on the CEO's leadership team. The conversations with the partners surprised me. Each one followed a familiar pattern. Their shock and disbelief at the choice, as I explained I wanted more time with my kids before confessing I had a growing disillusionment with the firm strategy and what it was doing to the culture. I felt we were endlessly chasing profit, and damaging the company culture in the process. Said more simply, I had a harder time justifying leaving my husband and kids to work 12-14 hours a day, flying away every week, all to simply, as one rising consultant put it, "make rich guys *richer*." I varied how much of the truth I told to each person depending on my level of trust, but the gist was: **I wanted more *life* in my life**.

To their credit, each and every person I shared with fell silent at my explanation. The responses were a combination of recognition and acknowledgment, that they had a similar point with their spouses years ago and had to make changes in their family dynamic. Or awe and maybe a little envy that they had wanted to do something about their situation earlier, but now felt it impossible to do so.

Most of the female partners told me they were the breadwinners and couldn't justify leaving to do anything else, while the men told me their wives had grown accustomed to their incomes and they now were somewhat "stuck" in a lifestyle, paying for private schools or colleges. Other clients and colleagues told me they were missing crucial years with their kids and didn't know how to prevent that, hoping Covid changes would stick and they'd limit travel and build new traditions. I heard from dads who confessed to missing the window with their children but were at least relieved to have built a great salary and savings to take the family to box seats at a baseball game. As if box seats would somehow replace the time they could have spent playing catch. Or the emotional investment they had missed giving them in those key development years. In both cases, they had chased financial security as the most important value rather than actually getting to live the life they were financing.

I totally understood their comments – and without judgment – because I had told myself those stories for a very long time. Up until the moment I quit, I was no different. I justified being miserable by telling myself that I wasn't. Telling myself I didn't have a choice. I had *chosen* this job, it helped pay for trips and college, and I should just put my head down and keep going. Stay in the game. *Who was I to feel unfulfilled when I was blessed with so much?* Quitting a well-paying job that I was great at and had organized a life around just didn't seem to be an option. But I'd hear that little voice telling me I was meant for something more than this. I thought that maybe when the kids grew up I'd get to join a board and do something that improved the world. And I found that throwing yourself into a 24/7 work pace is an effective way to silence that voice inside you. Little did I know it would find other ways to just speak louder.

The worst stories, the ones that made me instantly grateful for my decision, played out with partners ten years older than me, giving me a glimpse of my future if I had stayed on this trajectory. Several had just been unceremoniously let go after more than thirty years on the job. After moving their families every few years, giving their entire careers, and at the highest pay packages, these workers were now deemed *too expensive* to keep even if they were still producing…with only three years to go until retirement. Sure, they were paid out to leave. But the stories they shared were heartbreaking.

One had just gotten divorced and planned to finally move abroad in two years, but now with an early exit and COVID he was stuck home, alone. Another had planned to do something different in retirement, but assumed he had two more years to make connections and reposition himself in the market– now, he was left scrambling. A top leader who seemed to have it all was unsure of his next steps, including the status of his marriage and his living arrangements. A fourth told me his health really suffered from the lifestyle, and the pace and stress cost him about five years off his lifespan.

I instantly felt empathy, and saw my story reflected in theirs. But the harsh reality is that I, and they, always had a choice; we were just stuck inside a system that made us believe we didn't. Whether that was self-imposed from our own limiting beliefs, or just conveniently reinforced to keep everyone marching at the same pace towards a higher share price, I don't know. It probably depends on each person's story.

In the Recognize phase of Corporate Rehab, you'll start to examine your past and your story - life experiences, childhood, key relationships, trauma, personality - anything that could have helped to shape your worldview and values. We start at the beginning, because your world views and personality are stored in the subconscious and are shaped by age seven.[61] That's right: by first grade, you've decided how the world works, and unless you become aware of it, that perspective stays in the back of your mind, influencing your risk tolerance, who you marry, and what career you choose. This means that your family of origin and understanding your childhood could be fairly important to looking at why you believe the things you do. Though there are many aspects that make up your story; we'll cover just a few key themes here, including attachment theory, hierarchy of needs, and the impacts of trauma.

Attachment Theory

Research on early childhood attachment science shows that when children experience reliable bonds with caregivers, and receive dependable comfort under stress, they are freed to learn and develop instead of devoting energy to survival, or staying hypervigilant.[62] Attachment theory focuses on either secure attachment, or three types of *insecure* attachment: avoidant, ambivalent, or disorganized. In avoidant attachment, the

[61] Courtney E. Ackerman, MA. *What is Attachment Theory? Bowlby's 4 Stages Explained* (Positive Psychology blog, Apr 27 2018).
[62] Daniel Siegel and Dina Payne Bryson, *The Power of Showing Up* (Ballantine Books, 2021, p 29).

child's emotional needs are mostly ignored and, in turn, they have difficulty navigating their own internal set of emotions, and learn to be dismissive of emotional worlds and potential connections with others as a result. In the ambivalent attachment style, the child's caregiver was inconsistent - sometimes warm and attentive, other times unavailable or distracted - leading the child to feel anxious about whether your needs would be consistently met. In the disorganized attachment style, the child is exposed to intense fear, often from a parent themself, from behavior that was erratic, abusive or neglectful, confusing the child about when the parent could be relied upon to be safe, and staying hypervigilant to avoid behavior that would be frightening.

Attachment theory can be an important clue because your subconscious mind was shaped so early in life. How you bonded with caregivers, whether you learned if you could trust them, that you'd be nurtured when you cried, the presence of loud sounds, and how you learned to self-soothe all gave you signals about what the world was like, and whether you could trust the adults around you. These experiences also likely told you whether your own needs were important, which needs took priority, and how to get them met in either healthy or unhealthy ways.

Hardwired Hierarchy of Needs

You likely remember the concept of Maslow's hierarchy of needs from biology class, but I doubt many of us have reviewed it routinely to see where we stand on the arc from meeting basic needs to approaching self-actualization. There is a stark difference between the basic needs (safety, security, food, and water) and the psychological needs (belonging and esteem), before you get anywhere close to the top of the pyramid at self-actualization.

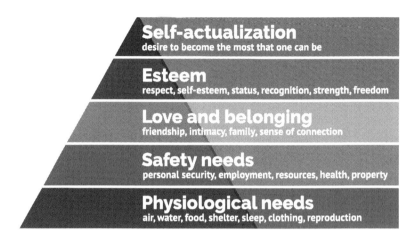

Maslow's Hierarchy of Needs

The concept is that humans are motivated by a hierarchy of needs, organized into a stacking set such that the more basic needs must be met before one can attend to the higher-order needs. The behavior associated with leading to self-actualization is clear in Maslow's description: trying new things instead of sticking to safe paths, listening to your own feelings instead of the voice of authority, being honest instead of playing games, being prepared to be unpopular if your views don't coincide with the majority, and having the courage to give up your defenses.[63]

Here's the rub: when you are hustling for your worth or stuck in a toxic culture, you do the *opposite* of what's on that list. You are encouraged to chase results that are a sure bet, not question authority or the strategy, play games to win, focus on individualized metrics, stick with the majority, and protect any of

[63] Saul McLeod, PhD, *Maslow's Hierarchy of Needs* (Simply Psychology blog, April 04, 2022)

your defenses so that you project confidence. You should appear strong, tough, or perfect. But to exhibit the behaviors of self-actualization at the top of the pyramid, you actually need to be *vulnerable*. Vulnerability is a trait that is absolutely crucial for connection and belonging, according to Brené Brown, but also something that will definitely get you eaten alive in corporate America (according to me and 98% of the women I spoke with; the other 2% don't live in America). So, after meeting your basic needs, the next level of needs you have - belonging and connectedness - require of you the one trait that you cannot safely exhibit at work. In the words of Aditi, a female executive, "guess what happens when you are vulnerable [in corporate America]... you will be devoured by the wolves."

Toxic cultures are often run by people operating at a lower level of needs, stuck in a culture of scarcity or survival mode running in their subconscious, and using financial security or success to replace the other higher level of needs, including connectedness and belonging, esteem, and self-actualization. But the higher order needs are the ones that women I spoke with desired the most. And a lot of the men too. When I surveyed fellow partners on my way out, all of the men said they'd gladly give back some of their salary if they could reclaim their time and their lives - have some more time with their family, or pick up a hobby. *What does that tell you?* The small teams at the top of today's corporate structures have made a tradeoff of financial security at the risk of other needs and are, at best, unaware of the impact of their choices, or at worst, aware and dictating that you do the same to feed the machine. Perhaps it's both.

On a run with a friend, I talked about just now realizing that I had been burying my needs for so long, and she quipped: "Do any of us know what our needs are? What are mine?" As if anyone could answer that but her. Many of us weren't raised with a sense of who we truly are or what we need. For many reasons. The bottom line: get in touch with your own needs, know where you are on the hierarchy of self-evolution, and look at how the leadership in your company, family, or community behaves relative to these priorities. If leaders are stuck in survival mode and exhibiting behaviors of meeting basic needs, ask yourself how you will grow if things continue to stay as they are.

Trauma and Intergenerational Trauma

Doctor and researcher Gabor Maté believes trauma isn't what happened in your lifetime, but that it's your individual *reaction* to what happened. As Oprah Winfrey and Dr. Bruce D. Perry explore in their book, *What Happened to You?*, the shift in understanding needs to move from someone's behavior to the underlying reason for the behavior.[64] According to a 2019 study by the U.S. Centers for Disease Control, 60% of American adults report having had at least one adverse childhood experience (ACE), which the researchers believe to be underestimated. The ACE study outlines eight key experiences associated with trauma. Recent studies distinguish between what is known as a simple, or one-time, trauma – like witnessing a car accident – and what is known as complex trauma, the sustained series of events, such as living with an alcoholic. In complex trauma, part of recognizing is understanding what the experience was like for you. In his book, Dr. Perry gives the example of a fire at an elementary school, in which a veteran firefighter realizes the flames are controllable and quickly extinguishes them. In contrast, a small child may experience fear, confusion, and helplessness as his classroom goes up in flames.[65] It's less important to agree on what was observed

---

[64] Oprah Winfrey and Dr. Bruce D. Perry, *What Happened to You*, (Flatiron Books, 2021)
[65] Ibid, p 101.

during the event, and more important to understand how each person experienced it themselves, and what coping mechanisms or stories they adopted in order to make sense of what was happening. As one therapist, Jean, quipped in my interviews: "Two people can witness the same event, and there will be three experiences: hers, his, and then what actually happened."

Knowing the majority of U.S. adults have experienced some form of trauma, it led me to this question: What happens to those basic and higher level needs in the presence of trauma? It can certainly interrupt a person's ability to identify needs and get them met, leaving emotional wounds that people may not even be aware of. When we do not get our basic needs met, we can learn to meet them in unhealthy ways. *Enter coping strategies.* Unfortunately, while many of these coping strategies will get you ahead in corporate America, they can also be dangerous in that environment without an off switch. Things like:

- Performing to earn praise: Maybe you throw yourself into work, believing the more you produce or perform, the better you are and the more value you provide. This works great for promotions; it's awful for living as a whole person and just fuels the hustle culture.

- Relaxing boundaries: Boundaries keep you safe, and can be physical, temporal, or mental. Anyone who is in a customer-facing role likely needs to get reacquainted with them, particularly if you are working across time zones or have team members working a combination of remote and physical office schedules.

- Numbing: Mentally checking out or drowning feelings of being overwhelmed, anxious, or frustrated through social media, substances like alcohol, or – my favorite for moms everywhere – what I like to call "Netflix and Numb."

And, if you were raised with scarcity, financial or emotional, who around you can help you navigate as you pursue both wholeness and ambition? Not your extended family who never expected you'd reach as high as you already have, and have no advice for how to navigate the top. Not your friends, who often have made the same choices and can't provide objectivity. Not your spouse, who often has a vested interest in you continuing to provide a lifestyle or financial security. So, the answer is: you. You're the only one who can tell yourself when you've achieved enough. But, if you've gotten this far, and sacrificed this much, chances are that you don't have self-awareness or the tools to make the right tradeoffs easily. So, what do you do? You silence that little voice, put your head down, and work harder.

Gabor Maté, a world-renowned physician and researcher on trauma, suggests that all mental illness and addiction actually has its roots in emotional loss or trauma. In his definition, it's not what happens to you externally that defines the trauma but what happens *internally* to you as a result of it. If the word trauma is a derivative of the Greek word for wounding, he suggests that your reaction to the trauma you experience is to separate from yourself; to form scar tissue that has been hardened, to use his metaphor. In response, people develop illness in their bodies, minds, and psyches or selves, which can show up as anxiety, depression, disease, or addiction to substances to numb the pain. To emphasize his point, his research found a connection between unexpressed anger and autoimmune diseases, noting that 80% of people with an autoimmune disease are women.[66]

The unfortunate thing about trauma is that it is passed down through generations, like an inheritance you never wanted and

---

[66] Gabor Mate, *In the Realm of Hungry Ghosts: Close Encounters with Addiction*, (North Atlantic Books, 2010).

cannot see. Things that ancestors may have endured caused them to develop values borne of circumstance and necessity, which they passed from generation to generation. As part of my healing journey, I started to dig into my background to understand where my mindset came from. They sound like internal soundtracks that say "do more," "run faster," or "you're not enough." The answer on where they came from as a woman in America is likely: everywhere. But some of it may have been handed down before we were even born.

My grandmother was a huge influence in my adolescence. One of eight kids, she was raised in a big Irish Catholic family in the coal mining mountains of Western Maryland. While she and her siblings survived The Great Depression and poverty, it certainly left its mark. The memories of sleeping three kids to a bed, one meal a day, and converting a house into a duplex to fit 16 people translated into a ton of wisdom dispensed from Grandma Louise, or Weezie, as she drove us around Maryland in her baby blue Pontiac. We'd listen to strong female protagonist country artists, like Dolly Parton, Crystal Gale, and Loretta Lynn, while Weezie dispensed nuggets of wisdom. Singing along to the radio, she'd turn it down every so often and toss out a line like, "if you work really hard, then one day you can afford a big house," or "it's always good to have options, girls - I didn't have those." There were also darker things, beyond our years, typically following the lyrics of those songs that only now as an adult do I understand: the backbreaking work of raising children, the tales of men drinking and wandering, and how women were supposed to hold the family together.

My grandmother had been the breadwinner, working as a telephone operator while her husband held down a myriad of jobs after the war. I never knew him as he died when my dad was 19, but even had he lived, I'm not sure I would have really *known* him. The men in my family tended to be stoic and unemotional; a sharp contrast to their Irish humor and huge personalities that came forth as the whiskey flowed. The reality was: life *was* hard. Weezie lived in times of real scarcity: from meat and money to emotions. There's little room for growth and taking on new perspectives when you are busy surviving. For both of my grandfathers who served in World War Two, allowing emotions in a war could get you killed. So they didn't. And they survived. But like so many men of that generation, at what cost to the families they came home to? What values and expectations did they pass along?

How to Recognize

We've covered how attachment theory, your hierarchy of needs, and trauma could be part of recognizing your story. Now, pause and think about your own experience, and write down anything that comes up for you:

1. Do you remember values about work or family being shared in your home? Were there discussions about the types of dreams you had, and how you'd manage and achieve those dreams? Did you observe your parents relaxing? Playing?

2. How do you think these perspectives impact who you are today, and which version of yourself you bring to work versus who shows up at home?

3. Can you relate to a time when you lost yourself, and got caught up in the hustle culture? Or felt a need to be productive? What was going on at the time, and what did it look like?

4. To start thinking about your purpose, use the Japanese approach, called Ikigai, which means "reason for being." Answer these four questions and imagine them as an overlapping Venn diagram: What do you love? What does the

world need? What can you be paid for? What are you good at? Now, what types of things are at the center of all four circles? We'll finalize this during our Build phase, but this exercise should help you start thinking.

In my coaching business, I have clients make a timeline of their life, aligned with the levels of fulfillment and frustration. Louise DeSalvo, an author and researcher who wrote *Writing as a Way of Healing*, says that one way to truly heal is to be able to articulate your own story.[67] The highs and lows, any pain or grief you've experienced, and also when you have been your happiest or most carefree. You're in the process of getting reacquainted with yourself. Next, we look at the roles you play or have played, and how you define success in each of them. We walk through how those moments shaped them, and recognize some of the limiting beliefs or patterns that they see repeating. Things like, I'm not enough, people are out to get me, emotions aren't useful, and I need to prove myself. As babies, we are not born believing these things; you have the power to understand where they came from, and then decide whether you want to continue to hold onto them, or replace them with something more true.

Now that you've begun to recognize your story and your past, let's take a look at your life today.

---

[67] Louise DeSalvo, *Writing as a Way of Healing: How Telling Our Stories Transforms Our Lives* (Beacon Press, 2000).

CHAPTER 6

EVALUATE: TELLING YOURSELF
THE TRUTH

"Those who do not move, do not notice their chains."

— **Rosa Luxemburg**

We went golfing as a family on a Sunday evening about six months into my healing journey, and the day itself was pretty relaxed. The agenda included a run through the woods with my husband, reading the paper with coffee, seeing friends, taking the doors off the Jeep and driving around town, bouncing on the trampoline, having dinner and attempting to golf nine holes with the kids. Probably the way Sundays are *meant* to be; filled with rest, relaxation, and fun.

But my old Sundays weren't like that. I went into what the kids called "Sunday mode," where all day I felt the pressures of the looming work week. Constantly waffling on whether to do some work and prep on Sunday nights to relieve the anxiety of not being prepared and to set up the week, or to reserve Sundays for my family to play and rest and enjoy. The result was a woman on edge. Desperately trying to relax and enjoy the time, but feeling pressure to get things done and be ready to go at 5:30 Monday morning - either with a 7 am flight, or a trip to the gym. I understand now why they call it the *Sunday Scaries*.

A tidal wave of conflicting emotions built up on those days. Pride and eager anticipation of the work week would bring me validation, in contrast to the looming loneliness that would accompany leaving my kids early in the morning. Plus the anxiety of where to focus my time, and the self-doubt that *maybe* this schedule isn't what I worked all those years to achieve. *Was this way of living the prize for all that sacrifice? Wasn't it supposed to feel good, or at least satisfying?* To deal with the messy emotions I was feeling, I sought to control the environment around me. Forcing everyone to have clean rooms and groceries and laundry done and backpacks packed and no to "just five more minutes" of TV. Planning down to the minute of waking up, my Uber pick up, exact route to the airport, TSA precheck– all to minimize the time spent away from my family. I was looking to control my time, but really I wanted more control in my life.

This particular Sunday felt too settled, too calm, and I found myself wondering if I needed to shake things up. I now know this is what happens in a dysregulated nervous system; no matter what is healthy for me, if things are too settled, I will seek chaos and then seek stability *from that chaos*. It's familiar. But that doesn't mean it's good for you. "[Stress causes a] natural high," Concordia University neuroscientist and addiction specialist Jim Pfaus explains.[68] "By activating our arousal and attention systems, stressors can also wake up the neural circuitry underlying wanting and craving — just like drugs do."

---

[68] Katherine Schreiber, *Can We Become Addicted to Stress?* (The Greatist blog, September 2012)

It shows up as adding more to the task list, squeezing in one more sport the kids want to play, saying 'yes' to more outings and events than you can actually fit into your day, and basically staying "on" all the time. I tried to stay in the moment and appreciate being out with my family; everyone was (pretty much) getting along, I was bonding with my preteen daughter, and I could relax and enjoy it. I didn't have to run from it or create chaos where none existed. Those patterns and coping mechanisms are like well-worn ski tracks going down a mountain, or a river flowing downhill. The skier or the water will seek the path of least resistance; the path that's well-traveled and known. Your anxious thoughts, or limiting beliefs, or the critical voice in your head. They keep recurring because they are *familiar*. But that doesn't mean they are healthy or good for you.

In the Evaluate phase of Corporate Rehab, you'll start to examine how stress impacts your brain and body, and take a look at the limiting beliefs, patterns, relationships, values and the culture in your current life.

Physiology & Limiting Beliefs

I am fascinated by the physiology of all this - how the mind and body actually work - in order to understand our reactions. The quick tutorial on physiology is that we have super old brains in our skulls that were useful when we were early mammals, and then newer parts of the brain added over time, like a house addition. The older parts (reptilian brain) help us with survival– things like fight, flight, freeze or fawn when you see a bear or witness a car accident. The newer additions to our brains help determine whether it is really a threat, and whether you have the resources to cope with it. It works like this: whatever we are experiencing is processed like a cloud of inputs - sound, sight, smell, past thoughts, new data - in the amygdala first, which regulates impulses. Then, that information gets routed to the hypothalamus (which acts as the command center) and then, a split second later, to the prefrontal cortex (or PFC, the thinking part of your brain). The whole thing works so amazingly well that your brain and body spring into action sometimes before your eyes and ears have finished taking in the scene.

It could look like this: you see a bear (hits the amygdala), you feel your body start to sweat and breath quickens (thanks, hypothalamus), then you calculate the distance and determine you can make it to your car (math, courtesy of your PFC), and finally your legs begin to sprint (flight). If you happened to be the same size as the bear, you could decide to approach it (fight), though I wouldn't recommend it. If you are a mom with babies in that situation, you may do that same math, decide you can't make it to a good hiding place, and thus exhausting all options, play dead (freeze) until the danger has passed. This wouldn't work with a bear, but there's one more response (fawn), that mostly women employ, where you de-escalate a situation with flattery or placating. Many of us learned as children or from bosses that appealing to ego was an effective means of survival.

The length of time it takes for information to move from the old part of the brain that regulates survival, to the new part of the brain that adds on thriving, can actually change based on how you've processed past events. If you grew up with fear and lack of safety surrounding you, your brain may get stuck at the amygdala, unable to move out of survival mode. In this case, the information is trying to be routed to the prefrontal cortex to tell you the danger isn't as dire as you initially thought. Turns out, that bear is just your boss asking for a last-minute proposal. But the receptors in the PFC that would normally accept that information are *turned off* by the trauma you experienced. The signals are firing, but nobody is there to receive and interpret them. *How does this work in your proposal scenario?* You are sweating, your mind is racing, but instead of starting to plan your next steps, you are stuck in a loop of overwhelming feelings you can't control, and feel like punching something or crying in the bathroom. If the signals were allowed to continue, they could move into the thinking brain but, instead, you may tell yourself that you should have planned for this, you are going to bomb this proposal, and it will cost you your job. And, by the way, all of this is running in your subconscious! You may not even be aware of it— like an app running in the background.

These subconscious patterns can turn into limiting beliefs that control us. These become the stories we tell ourselves. Ever had a boss who assumed everyone was out to get them? Seen a politician whipping up fear that outsiders are going to take what is rightfully yours? Noticed that your work challenges follow strikingly similar patterns, like colleagues who aren't team players or clients who underestimate you? Those may be stemming from limiting beliefs, and patterns that you're drawn to repeat. For female executives, they can sound like:

- "I don't think I'm experienced enough."
- "I need to earn more to feel secure."
- "I am not worthy of being loved."
- "I should avoid failure at all costs."
- "I should never question authority."
- "I have to win / I cannot lose."

Whatever is playing on that loop in your subconscious doesn't really care about the facts; your subconscious only acts on what you *feel*. And you will take on patterns to help you manage those beliefs you don't even realize are influencing your actions. *Feeling you're not enough?* Just check more off the task list! *Can't stand the narcissistic boss but keep choosing jobs where they surface?* Become the narcissist whisperer, and maybe *this* time you'll have the perfect response to prove yourself! *Feel drawn to scenarios where you can turn order into chaos?* Find a job where you can do that for a living! Yeah. Time to check those limiting beliefs and bring them from the subconscious into your thinking mind to decide if they are still serving you.

The Role of *Stress*

Beyond limiting beliefs, taking a look at your current life may help you understand whether your body may actually be *addicted* to stress hormones. Stress is part of our evolutionary fight-or-flight response and is the body's response to physical, mental, or emotional pressure.[69] One alternative to the fight-or-flight response has been linked to a higher incidence in women and called "tend-and-befriend," which refers to the inclination some women feel when faced with stress to tend their young and seek out social support.[70] Research suggests chronic stress contributes to many health problems, including irritable bowel disease, high blood pressure, the formation of artery-clogging deposits, and changes to the brain that may contribute to anxiety, depression, and addiction.[71] It is also a direct contributor to burnout, as we have covered. Stress in itself is not a bad thing, as long as it is in tolerable doses and limited in duration so your body can return to normal balance. The problem is when you are chronically

[69] Stress, (National Cancer Institute blog, 2022)
[70] Lauren McCarthy, *Evolutionary and Biochemical Explanations for a Unique Female Stress Response: Tend-and-Befriend*, (Rochester Institute of Technology, 2005).
[71] *Understanding the stress response*, (Harvard Medical School blog, July 6, 2020)

stressed, and hormones are being constantly released, wreaking havoc on your systems.

 "It took a pandemic for people to realize that their systems get overloaded just like a laptop does."

Relationships & Patterns

I'm not going to lie: this may be the hardest part of the whole journey. Esther Perel, a worldwide relationship expert, believes "the quality of our relationships determines the quality of our lives" - and she's not just talking about romantic partners. It's important to remember you are reconnecting to lost parts of yourself and building towards a future version of you, and not everyone will be excited about joining you on this journey. When I first heard that, I was hoping it meant your local Starbucks barista or long lost friends from high school. For me, there were some surprises about who was open to supporting me on the journey and who would prefer things stay the way they are. Keep in mind that this can be a lot of change, which is scary for others. How you've been showing up in the past may have worked very well for other people. You will need to decide on the level of honesty you want to face– for yourself and for those closest to you. And you are the only person who can make that decision.

The whole week leading up to leaving my job, the stars kept aligning. Not for some magical mystical "everything will be ok" but, rather, as direct signs from the universe that the relationships in my home needed some attention. First, a number of executives I knew were pressed to retire early due to corporate restructuring. Not knowing the circumstances, I reached out to congratulate them on their retirement. That's when the sad stories started rolling in.

Each one started with how much of a surprise it had been– they had no idea. Most were positive but a few well-placed comments let me know this was an impossible "choice" to be faced with. Leaders in their field, faces of companies within their communities, they moved their families across the country dutifully when asked, they'd taken last-minute flights for key meetings, took on one more project to help the company meet goals, and were undoubtedly told and felt that they were *essential*– now, they were tapped on the shoulder unceremoniously at 54 and told, "we don't need you anymore." What a slap in the face.

Then, the backstories. The wife who had just left him. The kids who had just finished high school and were already gone, and the wife at home he had to get to know again. The recent divorcée who never took the time to have kids and wanted to move abroad but was stuck here due to Covid-related travel restrictions. For each of the men, their career and identity had become inextricably linked. And, without warning, it was stripped from them. Yes, they were paid well– but what good is a full bank account if you've burned every meaningful relationship in the process... *and didn't even realize it?*

Those slaps in the face became part one of my wake up call. My husband and I took a walk that night, and he gave me some tough love in the midst of an emotional time for us both. "One day, Jennie, you'll be 54, and when they tap you on the shoulder, what will you come home to?" Ouch. It stung, but at the pace I was going, flying here and there three times a week, he was right. I hadn't been prioritizing authenticity in our relationship; assuming that our plan of having independent careers and looking away from the cracks on the surface would keep the trains running on time. I still loved him deeply, and back then I thought that success in relationships was avoiding conflict, so I should just ignore that something felt off, right?

Even worse, I began to really look at the lives of the executives, clients and colleagues I'd been modeling my career after. Judging by our conversations outside of work, each valued red wine, sports, and winning. Some spoke of their kids, but it was not the norm. All of us were unhealthy by some measure; the extra rounds of drinks and dinners on the road, plus 24/7 work schedules, catching up with each in our own way. Stories told at work included regular 5 am calls with the executive team, standing meetings on Saturday and Sunday; for many, there was literally no off switch. Did they get to enjoy the lives they worked so hard for? If I was looking to them as role models, what type of life would I end up with?

A few days later our neighbor dropped dead. We weren't close; I knew his wife but he was rarely home, a CEO of his own firm. And then he was gone. Overnight. As my daughter and I took a walk at the end of a remote school day, we passed his car and the still life I saw through the window made me profoundly sad. His papers were still strewn about the front seat of his car, a half drunk water bottle propped in the cup holder. Life: interrupted. I kept thinking, *what if I'm gone with no notice? Will I be proud of what I've done with my life? Or will I have big regrets?* And not the ones about never having been to a certain city, or gone skydiving. The ones that would align with my professed values, like, *did I show my children how much they mean to me? Does my husband know how much I wanted to spend time with him and felt guilty about flying away all those times? Does how I spent my days match up with how I wanted to spend my life?* And the resounding answer was no. Slap number two.

The final blow came from my teenager, my truth teller. The summer of 2020's pandemic schedule allowed me to trade being on 2-4 flights a week with taking up tennis as a family, and hitting the neighborhood pool in the late afternoons. I was pleased, smug, even, at how much we were getting to rediscover each other's lives. We had a lot of fights, to be sure, but we had togetherness in a way the four of us hadn't had in years. Or maybe never really had. Ten years ago, when my husband was training for residency, he was gone all the time. When he was home, he really did as much as he could with us. But there were many weekends when I cringed any time the phone rang while he was on call; he may need to dash away from us at a moment's notice. There were weddings and family gatherings I attended solo. Baby mealtimes and bath times delivered on my own. He was working for us, and for a future, but it still stung. And when he was home, he was not present, often sleeping or distracted. So, this newfound time, a decade later, with all of us in the house, rediscovering each other, was actually a gift. Punctuated by fights with kids over online school, a husband who had gone back to the office five weeks into the pandemic as an essential worker and me stressed out three floors away on work calls. But still, a gift.

But amidst the happiness of this backdrop, over the summer the kids had started to deliver lunch to me if I couldn't get away, or sometimes dinner. It was really sweet, but also left me bitter. Each week, more work piled up as the pandemic intensified, effectively shutting down my clients and forcing new plans to constantly be revised. For years, I had justified staying in this job so I could pursue my own dreams, but also to show my kids what a strong working woman looks like. One who has her own life and whose identity doesn't get subsumed in her children's or husband's needs. And then it happened. I had mentioned to my 12-year-old, as he was delivering lunch, how I was so happy we had this newfound time together. As you may remember, his response was, "Yeah, it was pretty fun! I mean, you were still on 12 hours of Zoom calls, but on the weekends it was a lot of fun!" Ooof. His comment was the third and final slap.

What was I doing all of this for? I started to acknowledge that while I was proud of myself for having reached the partner ranks, I wasn't really *happy* at work. I was *trying* to be happy. There were moments of validation, fulfillment, and excitement– but they didn't outweigh the burnout, exhaustion, and ever-increasing metrics that seemed to pervade our 60+ hour weeks.

Reconnecting with myself was probably the hardest relationship of all; I thought I knew who I was, but I didn't realize when limiting beliefs or old stories were running the show. As I woke up to my patterns, I had some eye-opening moments in both my work life and at home. I believe I am a warm person, but I'm also driven and ambitious– definitely not a pushover. And yet. When I resigned, I had agreed to leave my email open an additional month past my leave date, in case there were any leftover HR items that needed attention. On the morning I woke up without having to log in and start my Monday, I felt pretty free. Then I looked at my phone. What happened next was so ingrained that I never would have noticed it had I been rushing to start the week. I received an email from someone who didn't know I had left, asking me to approve a client press release on an account I had already turned over to another partner. My thought process in two seconds went like this: "I'll just go in and review it and approve it for him real quick; I wrote the draft and can do it really fast, and my colleague is busy with all I just left on his plate." As I hit reply, I caught myself. I don't even work here anymore. I was about to take it upon myself to do this man's job, that he was clearly capable of doing and well paid to complete, without it occurring to me that I didn't have to. Because I wanted to help, or maybe thought my time wasn't as important now that I wasn't being paid, or maybe that I could do it better and faster. Regardless of why, this mentality had trapped me in other people's agendas for way too long.

I recall vacationing with my family and going out for ice cream, as I was figuring out the rehab process. A small shop with limits on occupancy, I went in with my daughter to buy the cones, and was delighted they had my hard-to-find childhood favorite: black raspberry. They were out of my son's preferred chocolate and peanut butter, and I gambled buying another chocolate variety for him. I thought to myself, I'm the only one who likes fruity ice cream so maybe I should get another variety of chocolate for myself in case he doesn't like his. Again, I caught myself. At that moment, I realized how easy it is to lose yourself when you're just trying to love your people so well. I was choosing an ice cream I didn't even want, just to prevent my son from potential disappointment. My husband never would have considered that. I had to give myself a ton of grace for only doing this work now, realizing that evaluating and healing from old patterns would have also been hard with a baby on each hip, and while running on old stories as fuel.

Toxic Cultures & Your Values

In a toxic work environment, your ability to function at work or at home is at risk, along with your mental, emotional, and some-times physical health. The challenge is that, while there is some behavior we could all agree is toxic – like discrimination, assault, and fraud – toxic can mean different things to different people. It could include microaggressions, 'voluntary' work without pay, narcissism, bullies, jokes, backstabbing, or harassment. It could be feeling like you have to hide important parts of yourself in order to fit in.

> *"This is how the cycle continues: they take in young people, pay them little and tell them that this is the only way to do it; that there are no other options, nobody else will value them as much as you do, and then make HR an adversary and destroy trust."*

Donald and Charlie Sull have done important research in defining toxic cultures, and in their research of thousands of employee reports and surveys, found the five attributes that have the largest negative impact on how employees rate company culture. The Toxic Five include being disrespectful, non-inclusive, unethical, cutthroat, and abusive.[72] Their work examined the correlation between toxic work cultures and the Great Resignation, finding that there *was* indeed a link. In general, corporate culture is a much more reliable predictor of industry-adjusted attrition than how employees assess their compensation; it is 10.4 times more likely to contribute to turnover than compensation.[73] In fact, there have been numerous studies showing pay has only a *moderate* impact on employee turnover.[74]

---

[72] Donald Sull, Charles Sull, William Cipolli, and Caio Brighenti, *Why Every Leader Needs to Worry About Toxic Culture* (MIT Sloan Management Review, March 16, 2022)

[73] Donald Sull, Charles Sull, William Cipolli, and Caio Brighenti, *Toxic Culture Is Driving the Great Resignation* (MIT Sloan Management Review, March 16, 2022)

[74] A.L. Rubenstein, M.B. Eberly, T.W. Lee, et al., *Surveying the Forest: A Meta-Analysis, Moderator Investigation, and Future-Oriented Discussion of the Antecedents of Voluntary Employee Turnover*, Personnel Psychology 71, no. 1 (spring 2018): 23-65; and D.G. Allen, P.C. Bryant, and J.M. Vardaman, *Retaining Talent: Replacing Misconceptions With Evidence-Based Strategies*, Academy of Management Perspectives 24, no. 2 (May 2010): 48-64

"My lowest corporate moment was coming back from maternity leave and trying to fit meetings around my pumping schedule. My boss had gathered the rest of the team in the boardroom and announced, *"Diane is in the office, but she's dialed in so we don't have to listen to the breast pump."*

Toxic cultures cost both employees *and* employers. Injustice in the workplace raises the odds of employees suffering a major disease (including coronary disease, asthma, diabetes, and arthritis) by 35% to 55%.[75] By one estimate, employee turnover triggered by a toxic culture cost U.S. employers nearly $50 billion per year in 2019– *before the Great Resignation.* Not surprisingly, companies with a reputation for a healthy culture, including Southwest Airlines, Johnson & Johnson, Enterprise Rent-A-Car, and LinkedIn, experienced lower-than-average turnover during the first six months of the Great Resignation.[76]

Toxic cultures exhibit many of the same attributes as toxic masculinity, which is when men feel they need to conform to rigid gender norms, including bullying, dominance, aggression, winning at all costs, and restricting emotions except for anger and pride. Toxic masculinity is on display when men interrupt or talk over women, take an inflexible attitude, and navigate the workplace

[75] J. Goh, J. Pfeffer, and S. Zenios, *The Relationship Between Workplace Stressors and Mortality and Health Costs in the United States*, Management Science 62, no. 2 (February 2016): 608-628, table 3. Estimate based on odds ratio for self-reported physical illness and physician-diagnosed physical disease for an unfair workplace culture

[76] *The High Cost of a Toxic Workplace Culture: How Culture Impacts the Workforce — and the Bottom Line Report* (Alexandria, Virginia: Society for Human Resource Management, September 2019).

like a battle zone that must be conquered.[77] Take note, this is not "men" but rather "toxic masculinity."

"Too many leaders are unwilling to tackle male predatory behavior. When my company had a surge in sexual assault charges at employee functions and traced it back to alcohol as a factor, they didn't the remove the alcohol. They just stopped paying for it, so that they weren't liable for the consequences."

The key here is examining whether whatever culture you are in is leaving room for you to be living out the values you profess to prioritize. Do equality, trust, family balance, and integrity top your list? Does the way you spent your week or ran your last meeting align with those values? In my coaching practice we map out values and then align them to the percentage of time those values take up in a given week.

How to Evaluate

We've covered a lot of concepts, so this is one chapter that may take some time to sink in. Grab a pencil and ask yourself the following questions:

1. As you reflect on how the brain and body respond to stress, think about a time when you were super stressed; how did it show up in your body? How does it compare to now? What would you say to that person? Have you ever realized you were having a fight/flight/freeze/fawn response at work? How did that feel?

[77] Holly Althof, *How Toxic Masculinity is Ruining Your Workplace Culture.* (Alexandria, VA, SHRM, March 6, 2021.21

2. Start paying attention to your inner dialogue and the limiting beliefs you may be reinforcing; are there any themes that surface? Any ideas on where those statements come from? Are there beliefs that have overstayed their welcome that you can now set aside?

3. Are there patterns that tend to repeat, like working for an overbearing boss, taking on more than you can handle, or being unable to say no? Do you get bored when things shift from new or thought-provoking into steady and repeatable? Does it seem like you complain about the same scenarios, with only the names of the players changing? Do you find that you sometimes add chaos to your life when things are stable or boring?

4. Finally, looking at your relationships and your values, how do you want to spend your precious resources of time and energy? Are the values that are important to you (like family) reflected in where you spend your time? Are the things you value in your career (like growth, balance, or financial security) reflected in how you spend your days? What changes do you want to make? Are there small steps you could take this week to get started?

---CHAPTER 7---

HEAL: BURNING IT DOWN

*"Healing requires you to be vulnerable and strong
at the same time."*

- Brittany Burgunder

C allie was motivated to do it all. Armed with a shiny degree from a top school and a driven Midwestern work ethic, she snagged one of the coveted roles at her consumer products company, got married, and started a family. Moving abroad for her husband's job with two small children in tow, Callie began to distance herself from the driven pace and was able to see her role as just a job. Then, her husband lost his. She was thrust back into climbing her way back to the top, on planes from the time her son was in diapers until the end of elementary school. Exhausted and tired of the mind games, she realized her confidence had taken a beating in a culture where she says "you're only as good as your last mistake."

If you're looking for evidence of how gender plays a role in life, including career choices and society values, simply take a look at your local obituaries. Poring through the Sunday section on a cold winter morning, surrounded by my family and a roaring fire, my jaw dropped as I realized the pattern hidden amongst the smiling, faded photographs. The men's writeups went on endlessly about their work; the women's about their family. Granted, most of the dead were in their 80s; a generation where a career may not have been possible for the women.

I read page after page of the men's pursuits. One featured a full page ad starting with several paragraphs outlining the enormous deals he had closed just years before his demise. Another outlined the size of the company the man had built, his love for duck hunting, and how much he would be missed at the office. The final two lines included a comment about his four children and six grandchildren. With my newfound focus on the relationships in my life, I had to wonder, *did their executive assistants write those glowing summaries? Or was there a 55-year-old son or daughter dutifully penning what they knew of this father who delighted in deals and ducks, while they – his own family – were seemingly an afterthought?*

In contrast, the women's obituaries mostly focused on their families, or a love of cooking; the number of children she raised, where her grandchildren lived, and how she was famous for her peach pie. Sometimes a mention of who they had been before children, before grandchildren, before a war. But once they started a family, in contrast to the deals and ducks, their crowning achievements included children and cobbler. Neither is better or worse– but the contrast was *stark*. I guess if you want to know how to live, listen to what people say about themselves when they die.

But why is the work/life balance set up as an either/or, particularly for women? Choose the family or the career, but not both at the same time and certainly not in the same measure. *Says who?* I'll tell you: the men who felt they had to choose themselves, and chose work. They don't want to look at some of their painful life choices, so they double down on that decision, thereby setting the tone for others. They are working in cultures which reinforce these values and choices, and it becomes the norm. Anything that allows for more humanity or a broader scope of what you do with your life becomes the odd choice. And, conveniently, the people in these structures are led to believe that this is the best way, sometimes *the only way*. If you want financial security, you need to stay on a partner track. If you don't want to get "mommy tracked" and have people assume you can't hack it, then consider a shorter maternity leave.

When I was in Canada for a three-month leadership program, the firm gave my toddlers a book called, *How Full is Your Bucket?* The book teaches the lesson of how positive or negative remarks can have a big impact on your self-perception. You are supposed to balance what goes in the bucket, and fill it with healthy behaviors so that when you hit a sad or difficult time, you have some reserves. The illustrations included a sister whose brother constantly picked on her, spilling her cereal and getting scolded by mom, and a rain cloud following her around. My husband and I thought it was a great example for the kids of how to build a positive relationship with each other, but I never stopped to think, how full is my own bucket? And who or what was I filling it with? The irony of receiving this book for my children as I was the one leaving for three months wasn't lost on me.

My bucket was filled with hugs from my kids, date nights with my husband, the excitement of traveling, and respect from winning various work contracts. As my job grew, pulling me onto the road so often and away from nights with my husband and bedtimes with my children, the bucket grew too. Work demands and revenue targets made it even bigger from there. Frantic to fill it but not knowing how, I threw in all the wrong things. Excitement from travel turned into squeezing in *just one more trip*, eager to keep moving so I could feel that jolt of energy rather than the loneliness or pain of flying away from my family. Respect turned into a kind of validation I wasn't getting from home life, where the business suit was quickly exchanged for sweats and cleaning spaghetti spills.

And my relationship with my husband and kids? We tried to cram all the missed fun into full weekends, on soccer sidelines and dinners at cool new restaurants– but we missed the mark on *truly connecting* with each other. Travel, work, soccer, dinners, check, check, checkity check. But true connection? Prioritizing having a normal Wednesday night bedtime conversation in my marriage over the hit I got from closing another deal? Staying home on an uneventful taco Tuesday night, with no output to show for it except your presence? Those are the intangibles you can't really see. They don't go on a performance review. They don't give you that satisfying check to cross off your list. And, if you've had trauma in your life, your nervous system actually craves the choice that feeds whatever feels normal. And if chaos is normal to you, then chaos is what you'll continue to chase. The busy pace that feels fun but may actually be draining, the hit you get from social media likes that mimics dopamine you'd get from actual connection, the validation that makes you feel like you are enough if you didn't get that from a meaningful relationship. Mundane and normal interactions can seem boring to a dysregulated nervous system and you may not even realize that you are subconsciously drawn to drama or needing a full calendar at all times.

It got me thinking... are women actually taught to fill their own buckets? Because it seems we just look outside ourselves, filling other people's buckets – our partners, kids, bosses, etc. As women, do we even realize there's a bucket to fill for ourselves?

In the Heal phase of Corporate Rehab, we will start to explore how to heal your mind, body, and spirit. We'll cover the concepts of rewiring your brain and setting boundaries, and then discuss the tools of meditation, yoga, and other forms of healing for your body and spirit. Finally, meeting your needs in healthier ways. I must reiterate here that trauma makes this healing potentially harder, and a great trauma-informed therapist is an essential support structure as you go about this work.

Mind

Mind: Neuroplasticity

One of the most amazing things I learned is that science has only recently discovered the concept of neuroplasticity; we can rewire the circuits in our brains. I don't want to oversimplify this concept, but how hopeful is it that we can shift the design of our brains to learn new responses? The smallest building blocks of our brains – neurons – constantly send signals through our brains to our bodies. But you can reroute the signals by repeating an exercise in conjunction with a desired outcome and, over time, the neurons will form a physical connection. The concept is anecdotally known as "what fires together, wires together."[78] It's similar to what happens when you learn a new musical instrument; at first, you really have to concentrate on your finger placement on the piano, but after a ton of practice, your brain has formed a new neural pathway and is physically altered in the process. So, if you find yourself going to the same old stories or limiting beliefs, you can start small by reciting new mantras, leaving yourself sticky notes with the phrases you want your brain to learn, or practicing meditation.

---

[78] Forsyth, J., Bachman, P., Mathalon, D., Roach, B., & Asarnow, R. (2015). *Augmenting NMDA receptor signaling boosts experience-dependent neuroplasticity in the adult human brain.* (Proceedings of the National Academy of Sciences of the United States of America, 112(50),15331-15336. doi: 10.1073/pnas.1509262112)

Mind: Reprogramming Our Limiting Beliefs

We pick up limiting beliefs during all stages in life, but they are often rooted in childhood experiences. Once we recognize that these beliefs are present, we can choose to replace them with more accurate beliefs. Remember, *our thoughts may be real, but that doesn't make them true.* Holding onto limiting beliefs can prevent us from taking action. Working through your limiting beliefs can have a profoundly positive impact on your self-worth, confidence, and personal empowerment. To begin to reprogram and heal, I encourage women I work with to follow American psychologist Tara Brach's RAIN method: **R**ecognize, **A**llow, **I**nvestigate, **N**urture.[79] To *recognize,* first observe your thoughts (meditation can be very helpful here) so that you can catch yourself thinking a limiting belief. Then, allow those thoughts– don't judge them, just let them be. Next, *investigate* by saying that belief out loud and asking yourself if it's true. *Where is it really coming from?* Practice asking the five whys. Finally, *nurture* yourself and practice self-compassion. If not true, rephrase it and repeat the new mantra out loud.

The key takeaway is that after you identify and learn to meet your needs in healthy ways, you can re-architect the pathways in your brain to leave behind the negative self-talk and limiting beliefs, and begin to choose healthier interactions. You may have picked up these stories as a child; reconnecting with your inner child through meditation can be helpful in figuring out what some part of you would have wanted at that age.

Mind: Boundaries

Robyn, a former consultant, recalled how she didn't feel she had the right to set limits for when she'd do work or respond to emails. "If

---

[79] Tara Brach, *Blog – RAIN: A Practice of Radical Compassion* (Tara Brach Blog, Jan 1, 2020)

my partner worked into the evening, who am I to set a boundary?" While the rise of digital tools has made work more efficient, it's also erased natural limits in the process– particularly with remote work. The mental downtime of a commute, or shutting down at 6:30 because the parking garage was about to close, forced natural bookends to the day which remote work has erased.

In Nedra Glover Tawwab's book, *Set Boundaries, Find Peace*, she outlines six types of boundaries, the areas we typically need them most, and potential impacts of not setting them. She defines boundaries as "expectations and needs that help you feel safe and comfortable in your relationships." I now like to think of them as telling others the way you would like to be treated. I identified with this on a physical level: that person you'd rather not hug, or knowing when you need your own space from toddlers after being clung to all day long. But there are actually six types, including physical, sexual, intellectual, emotional, material, and time boundaries.[80]

In Tawwab's experience as a therapist, and in my own as a female executive, time boundaries are the hardest to keep– particularly for those of us who identify as "people pleasers." Tawwab defines time boundaries as how you manage your time, how you allow others to use it, and how you structure any free time. It may show up as overcommitting, performing favors for those who won't reciprocate, and prioritizing other people's needs before your own. As a working mother, prioritizing other people's needs was a way of life.

According to Tawwab, areas where we most need boundaries include family, work, romance, friendships, and technology. For

[80] Nedra Glover Tawwab, *Set Boundaries, Find Peace*, (Tarcher Perigee, 2021, pp 67-75).

the purposes of this book, we'll focus on work and technology, with a strong understanding that family systems are where your understanding of boundaries, or lack thereof, is formed. Unhealthy boundaries in one area tend to show up in others, like romantic or friend relationships. Work boundary issues could show up as taking on more than you can handle, not delegating, saying yes to things you don't have time to complete, or doing jobs intended for more than one person. You can contribute to not communicating or holding your own boundaries, but time boundaries can also be easily erased within the fabric of some work cultures based on cultural norms. Such as being offered vacation time but being chronically understaffed and unable to take it, being expected to respond to texts or emails outside of work hours, or being asked to postpone a vacation - particularly if you observe your leaders doing the same. Aliyah, a consultant, said of the work culture, "[it] actually rewarded a lack of boundaries. You gave more work (and sometimes the more coveted projects) to the person who always said 'yes,' and took advantage of the fact that they didn't have boundaries to tell you 'no.'"

When we don't set boundaries, the most typical result is burnout—when people become emotionally, mentally, or physically exhausted. Emily and Amelia Nagoski outline the causes in their book, *Burnout: The Secret to Unlocking the Stress Cycle*, as being directly linked to stress. According to WHO, burnout points to stress that is unmanaged, with root causes being a combination of exhaustion, cynicism, and feeling ineffective. And with female executives at highest risk for burnout, (in 2021 rates approached 50%) it's worth assessing whether you have the appropriate boundaries in place to prevent or stem the effects of burnout. Tawwab advises tuning into your emotions to determine what is causing you to give away your time, giving yourself permission to set limits, and teaching others how to treat you by communicating expectations. Often, this boils down to practicing a range of ways to say no. For example, *no, I won't be able to take on additional projects, I wish I could help but just don't have bandwidth, we won't be able to fit that into this week, I'm not sure I can get that done in the time frame - let's work together to reprioritize what's already on my plate.*

 "I still intend on winning, but I am going to win according to my rules. I will still hit your metrics, but it will be within my boundaries."

Body

As I waited for my annual health physical, I thought back to the prior year's stats. Back then, I had to sit and try not to get frustrated as I answered things like, "How often do you experience stress and anxiety?" and "Do you drink every day, or just a few times a week?" and "Do you ever feel like you're not getting enough sleep?" Is it bad to answer "every day" to each of those questions? How else does one survive young motherhood, a big job, and a full social life?

This year, I had some interesting responses. When my doctor asked if I was still experiencing stress and traveling a lot, I smiled as I was able to say, "Oh no, I quit." She stopped and looked up. "You quit? But... you're a partner. Nobody quits. In fact, I've been in this job for twelve years, seeing partners from all the different firms, and I've never seen one quit. *Ever.* In fact, they have...what's it called...golden handcuffs - so you can't." I just stared back and said, "Well, I did." It was super awkward.

Golden handcuffs. What an interesting term. She was right, of course. It was great money for the work. But the culture of overwhelm, the relentless focus on revenue above anything, and the lack of a strategy beyond share price - thereby missing the boat completely on innovation - was really the definition of selling out. It hit me that even if the handcuffs are made of gold...*you're still in handcuffs.*

And the personal toll? Her average patient is an executive male in his 50s, and this year she quipped that the biggest symptom her patients presented with following the pandemic was *divorce.* Many executives, who previously hadn't had to spend a lot of time with their spouse, suddenly found themselves in their company for 14 hours a day for 18 months. The unfortunate outcome was many couples found they didn't like each other very much anymore, or realized they didn't really know each other. In the doctor's observation, many partners "have more money than sense" and stayed on a track for so long chasing the things that would bring financial security, and maybe by extension safety, wholeness, or happiness. For others, it was a sense of identity; being an executive on a team with a perspective on a slice of the world or industry was core to who they were.

But the physical toll of stress was something many of the female executives I interviewed weren't fully in touch with. I started to notice a pattern as I interviewed them that many presented with physical ailments; so I began to ask whether they noticed if the job/stress had any physical impact on their bodies. Most demurred before sharing something they believed was obscure– only to realize how much it related to our discussion. I've already mentioned the woman who passed out and hit the drywall out of exhaustion, the woman who couldn't stop puking during the week, and the woman who was rushed to the ER thinking she was having a heart attack, only to realize it was "just" stress. Heart disease is still the number one killer of women in America, for good reason. Stress will leave its mark on the body one way or another.

If stress is so dangerous to women, what are the ways to heal? Sure, there's yoga, better nutrition, and learning to listen to your body (or not ignore it). But some of the women I spoke with took interesting approaches to their healing. Pam, an executive on the west coast, takes a proactive path when it comes to the impact of stress on her body. In order to stay healthy in corporate America, she believes "doing this lifestyle assumes a maintenance plan is needed. In order to keep my body acting like a machine, there's maintenance. If you pretend that doesn't exist, life will knock you between the eyes."

Pam understands that, when we keep our bodies in this level of stress, our nervous system actually believes and acts as though we're in battle. The body will increase activity in some places in the body, while it simultaneously shuts down operations where it can to preserve energy– such as the liver, hormones, and digestive functions. She works with her nutritionist to actively monitor her hormones and blood sugar to track how her body is functioning. Her best advice is to "check yourself before you wreck yourself."

Body: Self-Care

Ask a woman in her 30s or 40s if she is taking care of herself, and you'll usually be met with a confused look, followed by something off the spa menu of the beauty industry's definition of self-care. "Oh, I make sure I get my nails done/eyebrows waxed/new makeup/Botox/shopping spree!" But those activities are addressing your *external* presentation to the world, not your *internal* intrinsic motivators or human needs. Tuning into your own body through somatic therapies like breathwork, dance, meditation, or some forms of yoga are all ways to connect the internal experience in your mind to movement in the body.

Spirit

Remember Callie from the opening story? She decided to leave that company and move to another– but on her own terms this time. In addition to limiting travel, she began to lean on her faith to help her navigate what was important. All the messages in her church reminded her that you aren't defined by your title or your paycheck. She says, "God doesn't care if you're an SVP. Now I realize that you are *so much more* than your last mistake."

There are various ways to heal your spirit, whether it's therapy, yoga, faith, artistic expressions (poetry, singing) or something else. One friend went back to school for art therapy to handle her own trauma and switched careers to counsel others through theirs. Another is an ancestral healer who works with her clients to go back through their lineage to find an ancestor who was healed or is still wounded, and works to bring healing through the generations. Others practice yoga. As part of my healing, I took a yoga class on a beach in Hawaii from an instructor trained in Katonah Yoga, a Tao interpretation combining body, breath and mind, along with Chinese medicine and geometry. He focused on regions of the body that convey stored trauma (your back) versus openness (your front) and explained how unhealed trauma can show up as poor posture; literally people caving in their chest to protect their bodies.

Gratitude

Gratitude is also a powerful healing tool; a recognition of value independent of monetary worth. Generated from within, it has roots in evolutionary history in the survival value of helping others and receiving help. Studies have shown that acts of gratitude stimulate lasting impressions on the prefrontal cortex (PFC), making the person more in tune with future experiences of gratitude.[81] It's worth remembering here that the PFC acts in opposition and balance to the flight or fight response delivered by the amygdala. Working on a practice of gratitude can strengthen the executive functioning of your brain to intercept an amygdala hijack.

The Language of Emotions

It was a real surprise to me to discover that I didn't have a great sense of which emotions I was feeling during this process; I had always thought of myself as empathetic. But the language of emotion is something that needs to be *taught*. Often, we may know a word without truly understanding how it shows up in our bodies. For example, I always knew I hated conflict, but I didn't realize that I wasn't really aware of what I *feel* like when I am angry. Now, I can tell you that it shows up as irritation, typically accompanied by a tightness in my chest; I'm still doing the work to understand what my triggers are. Reading Brené Brown's *Atlas of the Heart* helped me to learn and label my emotions. In a survey she conducted of 7,000 participants, the average number of emotions people could name was three: happy, sad, and angry.[82] Getting a better sense of what I'm actually feeling has been a huge step in my own healing process, though that also meant I felt a roller coaster of emotions once I understood what I was feeling. That range included feeling terrified, elated, unburdened, lonely, lacking purpose, angry, bare, insecure, settled, inspired, resentful, curious, hopeful, peaceful, and joyful.

Feminine and Masculine Power

Balancing both feminine and masculine energy is key for women working in corporate America because we've been attuned to one

---

[81] *Gratitude* (Psychology Today blog accessed June 2022).
[82] Brene Brown. *Atlas of the Heart*, (Random House, 2021, p xxi).

way for so long in order to survive: masculine power. Energy, sometimes called prana, is the life force within you or the energetic layer of your being; what some would call your vibe or aura. We broadly identify feminine energy or power with nurturing, creation, openness, intuition, emotion, compassion, and community, while masculine power is associated with action, reason, logic, power, and strength.[83] Masculine and feminine energy are intended to operate in balance with each other, not *against* each other. Ancient texts from Confucianism, Daoism, and Chinese Buddhism call out the importance of balancing the relationship between the yin and yang, female and male. Tantric philosophy indicates that we have both of these energies within ourselves. In her book, *Woman Code*, hormone expert Alissa Vitti explains that "the universe is created by and made up of masculine (Shiva) and feminine (Shakti) energies that infuse all things. Both energies exist within each of us...learning how to engage both fully is what ends up making a person psychologically, emotionally, and physically well."[84] Dr. Claire Zammit's research on feminine power outlines an approach to tap *into* feminine power by focusing on three power centers: the relationship with yourself, with life, and with others.[85] For women pulled to take care of teams, create growth, and trust instincts, you can see how working in a system that values dominance, power, and strength could lead to identity confusion. You've been asked to set aside some of your greatest strengths within feminine energy, and focus on your masculine energy to get ahead. And that's not always the answer.

---

[83] Lena Schmidt, *How To Find The Balance Between Your Masculine & Feminine Energy*, (Chopra blog, May 31, 2019)
[84] Alisa Vitti, *Woman Code* (Harper Collins, 2014)
[85] Dr. Claire Zammit, *Feminine Power thesis* (University of California, 2017).

How To Heal

This chapter is crucial as healing takes time and can be a lifelong journey. But if you don't take the time now, I believe that old wounds or limiting patterns will come out another way. As Tim Ferriss so aptly states on his podcast by the same name, "your choice is: do you want to deal with it head on in the sunlight, or do you want to have it come oozing out of the corners in the darkness, where you can't contend with it in a direct or systematic way?"[86] The patterns could show up in the next job, your relationships, or be passed on to your children. It is extremely painful and challenging to be a cycle breaker, but you're paving the way for future generations.

 "It's freeing when your whole reality crumbles, but that can also be really scary."

Healing can take several forms. If this is new for you, a good place to start is by reconnecting with your inner child to heal any old wounds. This can feel a little 'out there,' but start with an inner child meditation, or by writing a letter to the versions of you who needed the wise counsel you now have to offer. The concept is that some version of you is trapped at the age you were at the time of various traumas. By communicating with that version of yourself, you can be there for her *now*, thereby releasing yourself from remaining stuck in the past.

Another approach to healing is to take the 'Mind, Body, Spirit' approach and explore things in each category to see which resonate with you. A great therapist I know likens the concepts that she

---

[86] The Tim Ferriss Show, Brene Brown, (Episode 409, March 13, 2020).

shares to a buffet table; where different perspectives, tools, and ideas may or may not feel right, and you're welcome to choose the things that do, leaving the rest behind.

Here are a few things to choose from the *Healing Buffet* to get you started:

Corporate Rehab Healing Buffet:

Mind   **Meditation** - My favorite apps for meditating include Headspace and Calm (for everyday) and Waking Up (for a bit more technique).

Mantras - Replacing limiting beliefs with truer statements. Place sticky notes around the house with key phrases. My family got rings and dog tags that say, "I am enough."

Future Self Journaling - This involves writing to the future version of yourself and what that more healed version of you might say to current-day you. For more on this, read *How to Do the Work*: Recognize Your Patterns, Heal from Your Past, and Create Your Self.

Inner Child work - This concept is rooted in the belief that there are multiple parts of ourselves, and one part could be the mindsets you took on as a child, which you can now help to heal.

Therapy - I cannot overemphasize the importance and need for therapy to be destigmatized and financially accessible in our culture so that everyone has access and the ability to heal alongside a professional.

Body   **Physical Movement** - Exercise, walking outside, yoga, dance - anything to get you out of your mind and into your body.

Nutrition & Sleep - Experiment with how technology can help, from apps to track nutrition to rings that evaluate your sleep. The role of food quality, water, hormones, chronic illness, and stress are all factors to dig into further with a health professional.

Emotional - Understanding how to label your own emotions is really emotional intelligence. Consult Brené Brown's *Atlas of the Heart* for a rich understanding of emotional language.

Breathwork - This can be Box Breathing that the Navy Seals do, toning the Vagus Nerve that runs through your body (if you have vasovagal and faint easily, look into this one!), or mindful breathing techniques.

Spirit   **Energy** - Reiki, acupuncture, chakras - there are all different ways to tune into your body's own energy and rhythms that we often ignore.

Spirituality - Anything that helps you focus on the relationship with your view of a creator - be that God, Universe, the Divine - can lead to deep insights on your next choices. Things like ancestral healing, spiritual mediums, and crystals help to keep an open mind.

Fun - Don't forget the powerful antidote that adventure, creativity, and joy can provide. Whether it's a poetry class, gardening, singing lessons, or learning guitar– it's important not to take yourself, or your healing, too seriously.

———CHAPTER 8———

ARISE: FROM THE ASHES

*"The midlife crisis for me was practicing law for ten years: **that** was an identity crisis."*

— Jen, a mid 40s mom/lawyer/lead singer in a rock band

I t strikes me that some of the only time I ever had to myself was when I was traveling for work. On a plane, out to dinner - I could decide where the team ate, when I worked out, what I did with my free time. I could read a magazine! That is, if I allowed myself to... after I finished an endless list of emails and work. So, unless the Wi-Fi was out or we were stuck on the tarmac with no access to a phone, I worked. *All the time.* In the plane, in the Uber, at the client site, on the way to dinner– until I was forced to put it down. At which point I'd shift into distraction mode. I filled *that* free time to the brim with team events and drinks. On the surface I thought I was making the most of the face time with the team, but underneath I now suspect it was so I wouldn't have to face my loneliness and confusion.

Of course, I didn't realize any of this at the time. I thought I was pursuing the "American dream." I was embodying the woman who had it all, showing my daughter and son what it meant to be an empowered woman with my own ambition. Wasn't this what our mothers had fought for? For the opportunity to be more in life than someone's wife, mother, or secretary? But something felt...*off*. The reward I got from work and hustling felt really good – like a hit – but it wasn't fulfilling and lasting in the way I thought it'd be. I thought I just needed to reach the next level, and perhaps then it would feel fulfilling. So, I put my head down and hustled harder, but more and more I couldn't reconcile some of my decisions.

I couldn't explain to myself why I was flying away from the three people I cared about the most. How this demonstration of being a corporate robot was supposed to inspire my daughter to enter the business world, or my son to support someone who wanted a career. Instead, I told myself that if I worked like crazy and got it done, THEN I could relax with my people. I kept checking things off the list during the week, so I could be free to join them on some nights and all weekend.

But a part of me realized that it didn't add up. Once I was home, I was doing all the home things: feeding, bathing, diapering, school form filling, volunteering - and, unfortunately, a lot of them were extremely mundane. I've now learned that normal or non-chaotic is healthy but back then it was quite a confusing equation:

- Get on a plane + fly away from your people + work 80 hour weeks + get fancy dinners and drinks + explore new places + meet new people + get validation from them = work.

  OR

- Do a more routine but less fulfilling eight-hour job + fix dinner + manage kids + manage childcare + manage school forms + exercise + keep house = home.

I didn't like the tradeoff of travel, but it felt like the only way I could stimulate my brain and get some validation of my effort was through my job. It never occurred to me that I could add leisure time or enjoyment into my non-work life. The list was never-ending, and any time I added some efficiency to free me up – a cleaning service, a live-in nanny – where did I put that extra newfound time? Not into play, growth, or relaxation. Because I felt guilty claiming it. I put it into the only place that told me I was doing enough, smart and creative, and actually exceeding expectations...work.

The Arise phase is all about growth but fair warning– it's that awkward cocoon stage between caterpillar and butterfly. You've realized the parts of your life that don't fit anymore, set aside old habits, and done some healing - *but what now?* Where should you point your North Star? Which direction is better? The challenge is nobody else can answer that for you. You have to do the work. It's easy when the path is well-trodden. But female executives have so few role models who have navigated the journey of working while female and being connected at home in a healthy or balanced way.

So many women I've worked with and spoken with have wistfully talked about figuring out their purpose, but have no idea how to do that or even where to begin. Often, it's because they don't really know themselves in the first place. They are a composite of their families of origin, lived experiences, and layers of conditioning that told them who they were supposed to be. Even from loving families. Even from their church. Even from their spouse. And *especially* from their jobs. So, to figure out what you're meant to do with your life - to ensure your purpose still fits - it starts with rediscovering yourself.

To Arise, we'll take this in three parts: know yourself, grow yourself, and show yourself.

Know Yourself

Reconnecting with yourself can be terrifying if you've been humming along, super successful in a version of you that is accepted and working well. But you probably wouldn't be reading this if you felt like everything was going according to plan. There's a reason you paused. So, start by asking yourself four key questions: Values: what do I stand for? Energy: what boosts me? Gifts: what do I have to offer and what are my strengths? Ego: what role is my sense of self playing?

Values

Values are "the principles that give our lives meaning and allow us to persevere through adversity," according to psychologists Barbara Markway and Celia Ampel in *The Self-Confidence Workbook*.[87] Your values are likely rooted in how you were raised, what experiences you've had, your faith, political affiliation, or socio-economic status. Noor, an apparel executive in her 30s, shared that it was only when she hit burnout that she realized she had been modeling her father's values of chasing success, rather than balancing that with finding happiness. While some values will remain the same throughout your life, the relative importance of others may fluctuate. Regardless of what they have been in the past, it's important to reassess– starting with a good list to choose from. Dr. Russ Harris includes a great list of values in his book, *The Confidence Gap*. These values include Family, Financial Security, Compassion, Health/Fitness, Nature, Accomplishment, Creativity, Dependability, Loyalty, Beauty, Bravery, Gratitude, Love, Connection/Relationships, Learning, Leadership, Survival, Self-Preservation, Security, Adventure, Work, Success, Calm, Freedom.[88]

---

[87] Meg Selig, *6 Ways to Discover and Choose Your Core Values* (Psychology Today blog, November 4, 2018).
[88] Russ Harris, *The Confidence Gap: A Guide to Overcoming Fear and Self-Doubt* (Trumpeter, November 2011).

Energy

Next, we'll look at energy. *What activities and which people boost you? What situations or people drain you? What types of activities did you enjoy as a kid?* Energy is increasingly being held up as a resource more precious than money or time. We usually know what it feels like to have a physical energy drain– but have you looked at your mental and emotional energy as well? Your mental energy can be strengthened by taking breaks, not multitasking, and listing out the activities that fuel or drain you - then managing your day with those things in mind. Emotional energy is tough for female executives because we typically come into work already somewhat depleted. The key is adding rest to your time outside of work– which most of us never saw our mothers model, much less our female mentors at work.

And if you are most influenced by the five people you spend the most time with, you'll need to avoid – wait for it – *the energy vampires.* These are people at work or in your daily life who suck the energy out of you. Before you say it's your children...I realize you can't avoid their needs, but this is where it becomes crucial to fill your own energy routinely so you aren't depleted when a tantrum strikes. Whether that tantrum is delivered by a kid at home or a colleague's ego in the workplace. Finally, time management coach Elizabeth Grace Saunders' advice is to manage your time and energy like money, by recognizing what your own style is: high drive, low drive, or fluctuating drive, and setting appropriate boundaries for how you use it.[89]

I'm still learning how to manage the energy part; it's incredibly hard for a recovering overachiever. Part of that comes from

---

[89] Elizabeth Grace Saunders, *4 Ways to Manage Your Energy More Effectively* (HBR blog, May 14, 2021).

wanting to be useful. Most of the women I coach have one phrase they use more than any other when we discuss what they want to do: they want to *help*. The team they are leaving behind, a mission-driven company, their community. Some of my poor energy management also came from my card-carrying status of lifelong people pleaser. My default setting was managing other people's needs, and to do that I'd often ignore my own energy. Becoming a new mom was probably when this nasty little habit got solidified; it was a survival tactic to not be in touch with how depleted I really was. I remember calling upon it time and again as a rising executive, and noticing that certain tasks or projects were a bore, but never really pausing to assess whether it was a specific person or type of activity that really seemed draining. To be fair, it didn't start with my newborns; I'd learned life was easier when you had fewer needs a long time ago. From my early upbringing, where my dad's mood dictated how your day went, to my husband's residency causing him to fall asleep at the dinner table, my coping mechanism to avoid conflict was to just try to be independent and self-reliant, also loosely translated into having few needs. It seemed easier that way. And in the short term, it was.

Gifts

Next, you'll want to examine your gifts. *What are you good at? What do others call on you for?* Gifts, or talents, are strengths that are innate abilities which typically have a strong biological loading, and may or may not be well-developed (e.g., intelligence, musical ability, athletic ability).[90] In his book, *The Healing Wisdom of Africa*, Malidoma Patrice Somé shares the two things that people

---

[90] Elaine Mead, *Personal Strengths Defined*, (Positive Psychology blog, 25 Mar 2020).

crave: "the full realization of their innate gifts, and to have these gifts approved, acknowledged, and confirmed. There are countless people in the West whose efforts are sadly wasted because they have no means of expressing their unique genius."[91]

Many people I interviewed were able to name their talents or strengths and women in particular understood the concepts of gifts or softer skills, but weren't quite able to label them. They weren't things that typically were measured for clear results, even if they had a big impact on the team or the project. I heard things like: "It's weird, I just have a sense of what the clients in the room want - I don't know whether it's by their body language or what they don't say, but I tend to know when they feel that something is off during the pitch." Sometimes this can be portrayed as female intuition; something in your gut telling you an answer you inherently know but can't always explain why or how. Scientists would tell us this is due to the gut-brain axis, where the two are connected via the vagus nerve and the brain has 100 billion neurons while the gut has 500 million.[92] Others would tell you that feminine and masculine power are very different - and intuition is something women can tap into as powerful creators.[93]

Other women shared that they had a gift in preserving the culture, and making sure that the team was getting enough development and being protected from toxic bosses. This is one area I found interesting, as the anecdotal evidence matched newly published research. Turns out that women typically shy away from the label

[91] Malidoma Patrice Somé, *The Healing Wisdom of Africa: Finding Life Purpose Through Nature, Ritual, and Community* (TarcherPerigee, 1999)

[92] Suzana Herculano-Houzel, *The Human Brain in Numbers: A Linearly Scaled-up Primate Brain*, (National Library of Medicine, Nov 9, 2009) and Emeran A. Mayer, *Gut feelings: the emerging biology of gut–brain communication* (National Library of Medicine, Jul 13, 2011).

[93] Dr. Claire Zammit thesis, *Feminine Power*.

of networking as it sounds too transactional, and fail to develop extensive networks external to the company (in the marketplace) but instead have superpowers when it comes to building community *inside* the company. They are more likely to build the team, support development, and contribute to activities that do not correspond to direct monetary reward, but *LESS* likely to know that they have options outside the company. This is why men tend to find it easier to get their next job outside of the company. It also sets up the average female executive to be more likely tasked with what Marianne Cooper terms "invisible work."[94] This could take the form of "office housework," like organizing a baby shower or a team outing, to leadership or management activities such as managing the culture and cohesion of the team.

The trick here is to start with the gifts or talents that you enjoy giving. Start with you. Then, you can layer on what your family needs, the company, or the world needs. Too often, I heard women describe what they wanted to do - even major in - in the context of what they knew would be feasible for a family, instead of starting with what met their own needs. You can begin by asking yourself, *what problems do I like to solve? What type of help do I enjoy giving?* Then, you can begin to match that to where your supply of help meets the demands of the world and the relationships that matter to you most.

Ego

One last note here that's pretty important in a male-dominated industry is debunking the concept of the ego as being a bad thing. Many women were taught as children that having an ego is *bad*. But the real definition of an ego is the part of the mind

---

[94] Marianne Cooper, *Research: Women Leaders Took on Even More Invisible Work During the Pandemic* (HBR, October 2021).

that is responsible for a sense of personal identity; that mediates between the conscious and the unconscious and is responsible for reality testing.[95] So, this is the part of you that you consider your "self." Which is a *good* thing, and necessary to get in touch with if you're going to know yourself. The challenge is when you allow that ego to overshadow other parts of your identity, or your authentic self. Some practitioners call this wounded ego your 'shadow self.' Nicole LePera has a great explanation for this in her book, *How to Do the Work*, where she outlines how we go from doing what comes instinctively as babies with no sense of shame or judgment, to getting feedback from others on what is considered right or wrong - from parents to school systems to work - and we adapt a persona in response. This persona (or shadow self) amplifies the things we get rewarded for, and downplays or hides the parts which we have learned will bring shame, judgment, or disappointment for others.

In my own life, I learned to amplify my achievements, performance, and task-conquering, and downplay my more sensitive side, including creative thinking, feelings, and intuition. None of those traits were rewarded: in my family of origin, in my academics, or in my work pursuits. And, yet, those are the areas I now understand to be incredible gifts, providing me with traits and talents that far exceed the value produced by checking more off my task list. My creative thinking helped invent new solutions in a pandemic. My superpower of being able to pay attention to the feelings in the room told me who the real decision maker was in a packed room of executives. And it was my intuition that told me something was off with my priorities and my lack of fulfillment in my job - but my shadow self /wounded ego showed up and told me to keep going. After all, who would I be if I stopped?

---

[95] Merriam Webster blog, accessed June 2022.

"The biggest thing for me was the ego attachment; that's where your identity is"

The shadow self is actually designed to protect the wounded parts of you. Its job is to keep you alive by hiding the parts of you that felt less loved and accepted. The confusion around your authentic self versus a wounded part of yourself is at the heart of identity confusion. Then, add on the roles we play – which for women mostly involve becoming smaller or more deferential to those around you – and now you're trying to figure out what part of you is showing up in several different situations. As mom, wife, friend, daughter, friend, church member, community member, and now executive: *Are you showing up authentically and just as you are in all these situations?* Or are you bringing a helpful, kind and nurturing version of yourself in some of these situations, and a conflict-avoidant, no-nonsense version of yourself in others? Would one set of situations be "life" and the other grouped into "work"? Now do you see why you need to address this, in the whole work/life balance discussion? In an effort to bring your *whole* self to work, you may struggle with understanding what exact parts are safe to bring, which you're even aware of, and which are most authentic or just personas you adopted. One executive, Dalia, shared with me that in order to excel at her previous job, she had to "put on a COO game face, and I would prefer not to be an actress."

Your Worth

A key element of knowing yourself is knowing your *worth*. Your self worth is not attached to a salary or title. It's not on the table regardless of your job. But often we're swept up in cultures where those lines get blurred. Maybe we were raised in a house where

performance was the way you got love. Grades, making the soccer team, or landing a good job were the ways you could secure
connection with your caregivers and feel good about yourself.
Maybe money was an issue, it represented opportunity, or was
treated as a shield to protect you from ever having to feel vulnerable. I cannot tell you the number of people who share that they
watched a parent struggle and decided they'd never feel that way
again, so the financial security of a well-paying job became more
important than a healthy one. Maybe you're working in a career
now where you're only as good as your last deal, or your identity
is extremely connected to that title or role. *Who are you without
it?* The bulk of the women in my coaching practice consistently
undersell themselves in their careers as well, not realizing the
depth of experience and the level of job they already qualify for.

If this sounds familiar, it will be important to separate your self-
worth from your career and to really understand what your skills
are worth in the marketplace, what you truly financially need
versus want, and how to value your time and impact. This sounds
straightforward but it can get tricky in practice. It requires you
to re-evaluate your commitments to yourself and your values
in light of new information, and realize that past decisions may
no longer be serving you. When I decided to leave and quit
abruptly, I got a few unsolicited offers immediately. Many were
in similar consulting firms for similar money and lifestyle, which
wouldn't have addressed the underlying issues. But one stands
out; it was for a creative job in a part of the country my husband
and I dreamed about living in, for about 75% of the hours I
was currently working, and about half the pay - but based on
the location it could have afforded us a very nice lifestyle. *My
immediate reaction?* I was insulted. How could they not see
what I was worth? Back then, I was still so swept up in the hustle
culture that it took me some time to realize what they had offered

was exactly what I claimed to want; I just needed to let go of the false idea that I had to hold out for a job that "paid me what I was worth," even if that came with all kinds of tradeoffs that simply weren't healthy for me. As a footnote, I'm proud to report that I help executives every day find roles that pay them the same or more– without the tradeoffs on culture or lifestyle, or new jobs that allow them to blend both. It's possible! It requires widening your perspective and redefining your worth.

Grow Yourself

The Importance of Play

We understand why play is so crucial for children, but why do we need it as adults? We need play, simply because it serves as an antidote to the sustained levels of stress coursing through our bodies in the 21st century. A quick review of the role hormones play in helping the body manage stress will help explain this. Playing releases endorphins, which are the body's natural painkillers, but they also work to lower stress and anxiety.[96] Hans Selye of McGill University named the fight-or-flight mechanism in his article *Nature* in 1936, and defined two types of "stress" — *eustress* (good stress) and *distress* (bad stress). Both types of stress release cortisol, which prepares your body to act — but there has to be a physical release of fight or flight. There's a great visual for this in *Burnout* by Emily and Amelia Nagoski, about a rabbit being chased by a bear. The rabbit will try to escape and, once clear of the danger, will vigorously shake its entire body to relieve itself of the stress of almost perishing. It's literally shaking out the cortisol. If this doesn't get discharged, cortisol levels build up in the blood, which can wreak havoc on your mind and body.

---

[96] Growth Engineering, *The Neuroscience of Games: 10 Ways Games Train Your Brain* (Medium, Jun 28, 2016).

So, if play triggers our bodies to release hormones to help us stay in balance, why don't we do it more? The number one answer I got to this question from women was, "I don't have time." Unfortunately, there are statistics to back this up. First, there are gender imbalances in leisure time. In a 2016 paper looking at these imbalances, Liana Sayer found that the time imbalance is split along gender lines. The labor statistics in America show that men get a half hour more of leisure time in a day as compared to American women. Doesn't sound like a lot, right? But that adds up to 3.5 hours per week, or 182 hours in a year – equivalent to a full month's worth of time![97] *Making matters worse?* When controlling for demographic factors, dads averaged an hour more of leisure in a day versus moms. *Ouch.*

"The gender gap in leisure is intertwined with college [education] because of the ways college increases paid work time … and also with marriage and parental status, which increase women's unpaid work more than they increase men's paid work," Sayer says. Women are working more, but their time spent on housework and child care over the last 50 years hasn't declined accordingly. And that leaves less time to play.

Second, many women responded with being driven to feel productive. Experts have coined the term "time anxiety" for being focused on the passage of time, and having it show up as cramming more things onto your to-do list, with worries about being late, or anger when time is wasted– even when it is beyond your control. Dr. Alex Lickerman, coauthor of *The Ten Worlds: The New Psychology of Happiness*, explains it as "when you base your happiness and

---

[97] Joe Pinsker, *What American Men Do With Their Extra Half Hour of Daily Leisure Time* (The Atlantic, Jan 7, 2019).

success on your ability to be purposeful, to add value in some way, you feel very unsafe just watching the seconds tick by."[98]

There's even an acronym for this phenomenon: FOND, or the Fear Of Not Doing. It's when you feel guilty spending free moments not being productive. The antidote, according to Dr. Lickerman, is to attach purpose to each of those moments. The downtime in the grocery store line can be reframed as planning out healthy dinners, or the actual playtime, like watching Netflix or taking walks can be recategorized as downtime to reset your brain after a week of nonstop performance.

And third, play isn't prioritized in our society. We've forgotten how because it isn't valued. If you're a mother, add on top of that a healthy dose of mommy guilt: any free time should be spent with your children. This may be the answer though - engaging in play *with* your children. One fellow partner and working mom explained her method to doing just that: she tries to fill her free time purposefully by building a Venn diagram where your free time, children, and any volunteering or giving back intersect. So, if she likes art, kids and volunteering, she'll sign herself and her kids up as docents at a museum, or volunteer for art night at their school.

As part of my process, I decided I'd never get this time back and if I didn't try things now to grow and play, when would I? So, I experimented. I tried surfing, learning guitar, bouncing on a trampoline, gardening, making wreaths, writing poetry, voice lessons, singing in a band, learning calligraphy, go-kart racing, meditating, painting class, travel, hiking, and making TikTok videos. And it was *really hard* to give myself the space to do

---

[98] Marissa Gainsburg, *I Always Feel Like I Have To Be Doing Something—Help!* (Women's Health magazine, September 3, 2019).

something "unproductive." But it was also incredibly freeing and hard to take yourself too seriously on a trampoline.

When I spoke to hundreds of women about this book, their own stories of play were fascinating, with a few stories of frustration thrown in. The amount of times a woman told me they had forgotten *how* to play or just never made time for it, was balanced by the myriad of ways others jumped in and tried new things. That rock band singer I introduced you to above? She was a lawyer for years, and then felt a rising anger with the state of the world in the pandemic, and so she did what any woman would do. She formed an angry moms rock band for other mothers looking for an outlet for their rage. One of her bandmates is admittedly more conservative, sharing that she doesn't look like a rock mom, but told herself, "why not just put yourself out there and take some chances, and do what makes you happy?"

Other women tried wakeboarding to bond with teenage sons, beginner's pickleball as an empty-nester in her 50s, a ropes course with young children, MudGirl runs with a 15-year-old teenager, competitive tennis as a break from a full-time role and two toddlers, becoming a comedienne on top of a government role, picking up a musical instrument she hadn't touched in years, trying out improv acting once a month after clocking out from a 9-5 job, and motorcycle drag racing for a mom of three.

Growth

As humans, we are meant to evolve; recognize that some of the angst you could be feeling is part of a message that you're ready for some kind of growth. We discussed the difference between a fixed and a growth mindset in Chapter 4, but to recap: a fixed mindset carries assumptions that your qualities cannot be changed, whereas a growth mindset supports an ability to improve and change. This is emphasized in learning approaches for children but applies to adults in our openness to change and grow as people.

This extends to people's ability to generate new brain cells, a process called *neurogenesis*. In 2013, researchers discovered that older adults could produce about 700 new neurons daily in the hippocampus region, the area of the brain that coordinates learning, keeps long-term memory, and controls emotions.[99] We usually hear these statistics associated with preventing negative outcomes in brain atrophy, such as Alzheimer's, but the same guidance applies to producing positive outcomes in feeling purpose and meaning in how your time is spent. And the further you move up in your career, it could be harder to continue to grow new skills or make room for big shifts in mindset, as management responsibilities take up more of your time.

Erin, a friend from college, had stuck with her consultant job through her early thirties, but found that the balance got harder with each pregnancy, and left the workforce after having her third child. Ten years went by, and she found herself wanting to do something that was just for her own enjoyment. So, at a friend's suggestion, she took up commercial modeling in her 40s. A few years later, she now has regular photo shoots in New York, and still makes it home in time to run the lacrosse carpool. On her time, and her terms. Another executive, Monica, lamented that she knew what would help her career grow, but had no idea what to do for her own personal growth. Another executive, Felicia, decided to get certified as a mindfulness instructor to balance her own mental health and enjoy the benefits of teaching others if she was going to keep her fast-paced day job.

---

[99] *3 Ways to Improve Brain Power* (Ameritas blog, March 21, 2017).

Habits

Part of reconnecting with yourself is learning to trust yourself. Your gut, your thoughts, your ideas, and listening to your own wants and needs. This is particularly true if trauma, gaslighting, or working around narcissists has been a reality for you. Psychologist Nicole LePera has advice on getting started down this path: keep one small promise to yourself each day, such as starting your day with a glass of water. I start with five minutes of my own form of meditation, which includes prayer and gratitude for the day and staying open to the lessons it contains. I cringe thinking about it, but the way I used to start my day was sometimes a rushed prayer, but always gearing up for the list of all that had to get done. If I had been in touch with my own feelings and thoughts, I might have realized it was anxiety and fear running the show, and it was an exhausting way to live.

When you have small humans depending on you, you've overloaded your plate, and everyone at work just wants more, it can be tough to see through the fog of habits and patterns you've fallen into. Author James Clear has great advice in his book, *Atomic Habits*, where he emphasizes that small meaningful steps daily add up to profound changes over time. Interestingly, he states that the first step towards better habits is found not in action, but in *identity*. He writes, "The most effective way to change your habits is to focus not on what you want to achieve, but who you want to become."[100] If you want to become a person who is more lean, then choose a habit like weight lifting, and achieve the outcome of lower weight. Instead of focusing on the habit first, then the outcome, and then the version of yourself you wish to become.

---

[100] James Clear, *Atomic Habits* (Avery, 2018).

Passion

Sometimes it is hard to find the things you feel a strong pull towards. We're accustomed to what our roles are, what we get paid for, what we know about, but rarely asked what problems or topics we feel passionately about. For women, and mothers in particular, hobbies seem like a distant memory. It's rare to find a working mother who actively has a hobby she pursues just for pure pleasure and not some sort of self-improvement, such as pampering or exercise. One woman shared that she calls her job both her work and her hobby because it consumes the time she would have spent on recreation. For many, we were raised to believe time for yourself to just enjoy is at best, a luxury, and at worst, selfish.

As one woman shared with me, "watching Netflix is not a hobby" so she decided to learn photography, and now donates her services to a non-profit. Another, Kay, a government lawyer, decided to try her hand at comedy and now has a regular stand up gig; a great creative outlet and contrast to her steady job and role as wife and mom. A Manhattan lawyer, Ruby, decided to dedicate a portion of her business towards supporting female entrepreneurs, and does a lot of the work pro bono. Other women began gardening, taught themselves interior design, got certified in yoga, and took up surfing– even in their fifties.

So many of the executives I interviewed really lost touch with the things that made them feel alive. In those spaces, they had filled in family obligations or more work, or outings with friends and exercising. But they forgot what they used to enjoy. A lot of this work is about remembering who you were, and still are, under years of coping strategies and obligations. Plus, the person and interests you have grown into.

Show Yourself

Showing yourself can be really hard for some of us. Once you've spent some solo time getting reacquainted with what makes you come alive and what patterns you have regarding early conditioning or coping mechanisms, now's the time to step into your own power. This can get a little complicated if you've had experiences where that has been threatening or unwelcome to others.

The things I heard most often in my interviews that hold women back from showing themselves as they are included being perceived as "too much" or "not enough," being afraid of both failure and of success, and wanting to step into their own power but being afraid of taking up too much space. This fear of both failure and success is linked to underlying fears of a narrowly defined version of success, and self-doubt about your own abilities.[101] People who are afraid of both could become paralyzed by decisions, or they could exhibit fear of each at different times. As an adult, I'd generally describe myself as confident, but I do recall feeling the twin pull of fear of making a mistake and failing, and also the feeling of being perceived as overconfident or boastful.

These comments are full of paradoxes, which you can trace right back to this elusive "likability trap" as Alicia Menendez' book on the topic so aptly named it. Being a woman in corporate America requires being strong enough to lead, but soft enough to not threaten others. She calls it the "Goldilocks Conundrum" where women at work are rarely 'just right' but often labeled too much or

---

[101] Sharon Martin, *Is it Fear of Failure or Fear of Success?* (Psych Central blog, Jan 19, 2016)

too little. What is expected of women - *warmth* - is perceived to be the opposite of what is required of a leader - *ambition*.[102]

So, how do you navigate this dilemma, when being yourself could cost you the promotion, but playing the game could cost you your authenticity? First, figure out your own style to balance warmth and strength. Mine is humor and a genuine interest in people's stories and outcomes, balanced with some honest questions or ideas. Sometimes I disarm with authentic charm and humor and then make my point; other times, I lead with the idea and soften the delivery with a genuine desire to get input and collaboration from others. For me, the key is understanding the *why* behind my behavior. When I feel the need to balance delivery to include others, versus when I'm being tempted to play small. As my daughter reminds me when I talk about my own experience, "nobody knows you better than you." And after more than forty years and a lot of work on myself, that is finally a true statement.

Taking Up Space

You need to understand context and your own style, but playing small does not serve the world. Own your strengths and step into the power of your own self-awareness. This looks like playing the main character in your own life, and looking inward for the answers before you look around you. It looks like knowing your own needs and prioritizing them alongside others. Dr. Anna Fels, a psychiatrist at Cornell University, interviewed successful women about their careers and lives, noticing "they refused to claim a central, purposeful place in their own stories, eagerly shifting the credit elsewhere and shunning recognition."[103] For women, and moms especially, this may be a pattern you learned from other

---

[102] Alicia Menendez, *The Likability Trap*, (Harper Business, 2019, p 33-35).
[103] Anna Fels, *Do Women Lack Ambition?* (HBR magazine, April 2004)

women, or it may be conditioning from typical gender roles. You may naturally, or from years of repetition, look to what others need before you consider your own needs, let alone prioritize them.

My journey to take up space probably began at several points in my career where I sought to speak more truthfully, but coalesced in my final year as a partner, where I began to call out the jokes, the gaslighting, or the inappropriate comments. Like the call with 100 people in attendance that I was running, where a male colleague said of a tough problem, "let's look under the skirt." I decided to call it out, realizing that if I remained silent in front of other colleagues, male or female, I was saying that the comments were okay. And they were not. Sandra, a media executive, shared her story about taking up space in her own way when she questioned the strength of the team, and then let the silence just sit there, unfilled. *For two minutes.* Another example is Deborah, who wanted the top CMO role but wasn't being given opportunities, so she directly asked for the job she wanted. She was told it would be another two years and then they would hire someone outside of the company. That bold move of asking for what she wanted made her realize she had been waiting for something that would never happen, and gave her the jolt she needed to fly 2,000 miles to a new town with her young son to start over in a new job that provides tons of growth opportunities. She now realizes how unhealthy the politics were in her old company, which she tolerated while dutifully awaiting her turn for a role she was never going to get.

My own mother shared a story in elementary school that I've never forgotten. She ran for class president in sixth grade but didn't want to seem unkind, so when it was time to cast the votes, she cast hers for her opponent. And lost by one vote. So, I'm reminding you now: you can be kind, but don't forget to bet on yourself.

Women Supporting Women

Finally, pay it forward and support other women. Those coming behind you, and those to your left and right as they navigate similar questions or build their own businesses and careers. And even those ahead of you, who may be pretty isolated and entrenched in their decisions and have a lot of wisdom, not to mention political capital, to share. I started a group chat including women across levels in my last job, just to cheer each other on and share triumphs with each other; one that I hear is still going strong today. Alison, a non profit executive, put together wine and networking for women at different breweries and vineyards each month. Soon after I left my job, I joined *Chief*, the largest women's networking group in the country, and then put together a local book club with a fellow coach committed to helping other women grow. One healthcare executive, Monica, shared that, sometimes, it's other women who don't want you to outshine them. Those women are operating from a scarcity mindset. There's so much work to be done to help women be leaders in their own lives, that there's plenty of room at the table for all of us. Here's what I learned from my own process of reconnecting with myself and my strengths:

Lesson 1: Be patient and give yourself grace. You're both reconnecting with yourself from the past and rebuilding your identity moving forward. This stage in the process is bound to get confusing. But it's also an opportunity to give yourself permission to have fun. So for anyone wondering how they get off the hamster wheel: you're not crazy. You can't do it all. So stop trying. Figure out what to let go of, and realize that you have the right to enjoyment in life. Just as much as anyone else.

Lesson 2: Experimenting with play was a great diagnostic for falling back in love with things that bring me energy, and pointing out where I wanted to grow. I had individual lessons from each thing I tried; many around the freedom that came from not having to assign productivity to an activity once I shed that hustle culture habit. Collectively, I also noticed themes: I tend to get reinvigorated by nature, pure challenge, and creating things - especially things that bring joy, comfort, or growth to others. As much as I was now aware of taking risks and being authentic and trying new things, when it came time to demonstrate that, I was as scared as any of my coaching clients. And this time I really tried to notice where I could feel that in my body and the messages I could learn.

I gradually noticed that areas of growth were in places that brought worries of failure, not being in control, or making a fool of myself. Like the time I signed up for adult women's hockey. At the first game, I got so anxious that I'd hold the other women back with my awful skating, that my ten-year-old had to give me a pep talk. So to chart my next steps, I wanted to choose something that would allow me to create something with some challenge that would benefit others, while overcoming fears of failure, imperfection, and loss of control. Nothing like adult ice hockey with women who competed in college to at least check a few of those boxes. Yvonne told me she felt the same with the rock band she had joined; it seemed intimidating but something told her to give it a try. She now relies on the band as a creative outlet and space to tap into deeper emotions than what she can explore between her cubicle and the carpool lane.

Lesson 3: Pace yourself. You need to carve out time for growth. Whether it is a company or your own human evolution. Except that women don't get much leisure time, let alone growth; you need to block it as an appointment on your calendar or get a friend or coach to hold you accountable. Organize the things you want to do and change into the categories of Mind, Body, and Spirit. You can only do so much at one time and part of growing is pacing out the growth so you don't get burned out on self-help. In the next chapter, we'll talk about making it *real*. For now, we're dreaming about what that growth could look like, and not taking on too much at once.

How to Arise

1. To find out what will help you grow or play, ask yourself these questions: When was the last time I felt like I learned something new? What activities can replicate that feeling? What activities gave me energy? What activities drain me? What do you like to do for fun?

2. What hobby have you always wanted to try?

3. MIT Professor Edgar Schein's Career Anchors test is a great one to re-evaluate the relative ranking of the things that matter to you as you progress. It centers around the level of autonomy, being a generalist vs. specialist, whether a title or span of control is more important to you, and the relative rank of things like security, family, and creativity. It's important to revisit these and ask yourself a few key questions on ranking their relative importance– particularly after going through personal or professional change.

Now that you are getting to know yourself better, what you love to do, and what brings you energy, you're ready to declare your purpose and begin to build.

CHAPTER 9

BUILD: BEGIN AGAIN

"I hope you live a life you're proud of and if you find that you're not, I hope you have the strength to start all over again."

— Eric Roth, The Curious Case of Benjamin Button

In a room full of baggy white shirts, one of these things was not like the others. My boss had insisted we attend a private dinner for our company leaders from all over the world, and I wound up talking with a colleague at one end of the room whom I hadn't seen in a few years. The chimes sounded for us to take our places, and I turned around...only to see the full group seated and realize I was the only woman in the room. At an international conference, in a room full of 80 global leaders from our company, I was the lone female partner. *How could that be? And how had I not noticed?*

The baggy shirts became a joke I would tell others whenever I walked into rooms that were sorely underrepresented. A joke that wasn't actually very funny. I told a few fellow partners that night how uncomfortable it was to be the only woman. The rest of that year, I'd get texts from the colleagues I had told, whenever they walked into a meeting of all men, "Whoa, I'm totally at a 'Baggy White Shirt' meeting." It was obvious they had never noticed the small number of women in the room. But once you saw it, it was hard to *unsee*.

It happened again when I was promoted to the leadership team for my business unit. I knew I was the only female partner on the leadership team, but we had female HR and diversity representatives who joined all the meetings, so it was easy to forget. Until we had our annual meeting to approve pay raises for each partner, and had to ask others to leave the room. Again, I was the last woman standing.

So much has been studied as to why there weren't more women in those rooms. The shrinking pool of talent for male-driven industries, women opting out to have kids right at the time their careers and salaries would have soared, the lack of mentorship or sponsorship. And for all the discussions on how diversity makes things equitable, we can also look at the financial benefits: higher rates of return when more diversity is present. According to a study by consulting firm BCG, women-led venture capital funds generate 78 cents for every dollar of funding, whereas male-founded startups generate only 31 cents[104] and McKinsey reports that diverse companies are 33% more likely to have greater financial returns than less diverse peers.[105]

There are countless stories of everyday comments that keep women from these rooms - either from discrimination or more subtle hints of not being welcome. That time a boss told me I

[104] Katie Abouzahr, Matt Krentz, John Harthorne, and Frances Brooks Taplett. *Why Women-Owned Startups Are a Better Bet*, (BCG, June 6, 2018)
[105] Vivian Hunt, Dennis Layton, and Sara Prince, *Why Diversity Matters*, (McKinsey & Co., Jan 2015)

wasn't invited to the drinks after the pitch "because I was a girl." Every woman in a company has a story like this one, but what was even crazier was my reaction: *relief.* I felt like my gender had to be the reason because I had nailed the presentation that day, I led the team well, the clients respected me— *what else could it have been?* My reaction was not anger. Not indignation. Not even a question of whether these were the people to whom I wanted to attach my career hopes and dreams. Just relief. I wasn't crazy; I *was* being treated differently and someone finally admitted it. He later apologized, but the damage was done. I often wonder what made him realize it and apologize. Did he tuck in his 8-year-old daughter that night, and think about how she would feel in my shoes? Did he have the same career ambitions for her?

But for all this focus on diversifying, nobody had really explored if women even *want* to be in these types of rooms anymore. Why would women, of any color, choose to slog through a culture as toxic as this or a game that feels stacked against them? Why try to fit into a room of baggy white shirts, when you're rocking heels?

In the upper hallways of corporate America, we promote (mostly) men into positions where they are forced to choose between endless work demands and family, and in order to rise, they choose work. And then we watch as they put so much into their careers that they lose themselves and their identities in their jobs - often losing the quality of their relationships in the process or dying shortly after they retire. Then we are surprised when the divorced male in his fifties, who is running the place, makes decisions for the company that are in line with his own life choices of choosing work first and crediting the hustle culture for his success. Instead of choices that could create a profitable company that promotes some balance or purpose for their employees. *What would those decisions look like if more women were in the room? Or more men and women who believed there could be another way?* To pursue profit, yes, but also include balance and purpose. And what would be the quality, not only of the revenue, but of all the decisions, if there were more women at the table?

But it's actually a false dichotomy - this choice between work and life. In reality, I have interviewed countless women who have found financial security and purpose outside of an office. It can be both - as long as you are making conscious decisions. There's Meena, the former investment banker who opted out after baby number three and spent years raising kids while quietly starting her own VC fund. Fast forward through countless bake sales and capital rounds later, and she has made more money on her own than she ever would have stuck inside a matrix that told her she had to choose. Brianna, the consultant who left, disgruntled with the lack of balance and opened her own organization for female entrepreneurs. Robin, the corporate litigator turned lead Peloton instructor, building a brand while building a life.

It may be a breakthrough moment to be the *first* woman in the room. But by the math, that means that thousands of women in your same age and situation have already opted out. You may be the first for the crop behind you - but for your peers, you were the last one who held out. Who stayed playing in a game you may not be able to win. As you climb the corporate ladder, and shatter the glass ceiling, it's a hollow victory when you're the only woman in the room. Or even worse - the last woman standing. *What did you sacrifice to get there? Did you make it to the top of the ladder only to find the ladder was leading to a room you no longer wanted to be in? Or do you now have an opportunity to build a bigger room?* Shelley Zalis, whose work with the Female Quotient I greatly admire, started changing those rooms full of baggy white shirts by creating the Equality Lounge, a space at mostly male-dominated conferences and events for women to discuss gender equity. Her work has created community and shone a bright light on these women's lived experiences in the workplace.

In the Build phase, you're building new dimensions of your life and career intentionally around your purpose, values, and priorities. This requires three major steps:

1. *Declare your bold vision*: your purpose, values, and priorities.
2. *Gather your crew*: build a support network to hold you accountable to it.
3. *Chart a course*: construct a roadmap of the key steps you'll need to realize the vision.

Declare Your Bold Vision

Creating a future vision for your life can be done in a number of ways: manifesting joy, praying, a vision board, a vision statement for a company, or even writing your ideal obituary. All the previous steps have led you here: you know yourself, your patterns, your priorities, your play, and now; your purpose. Think about your values, priorities, your why, your unique gifts, yourself, and create a vision of the life you want. How do you spend your time? How do people describe you? How do you *want* to be described?

If you've been following along with the steps in the REHAB framework, this is where I work with clients to declare their why; their purpose. It's typically written as: "to [action that feels compelling], so that([impact]." For example, your purpose might be: "to build technology solutions so that I can bring education to others," or "to operate as a healed executive so that I can make the most impact in healthcare communities." I then have them write their vision of their lives, one year from now– writing as if it has *already* happened. Funny trick with our brains: what we tell ourselves becomes truth to our brains; our minds cannot tell the difference between a phrase you want to be true and a phrase that is already true. So, if you tell yourself you're strong, you're not afraid, you're wildly successful, then your brain will shift into that energy or behave as if it is true. Remember this concept that we introduced earlier, "what fires together, wires together"? We write the future vision as if it has already happened: you landed that job that gave you more balance, you rebuilt that relationship with your teenager, you exceeded the financial goals you had, or you are now more calm and settled.

Back to that golfing story from Chapter One, six months into my healing journey. I turned to the kids as the sun set and told them how happy I was to be there with them on a Sunday night instead of at home making everyone crazy and getting ready to fly out the next day. They ran over and hugged me, and my son said, "We really like this new version of you mom - in the last year you've become a different person, and we love it." Even my daughter, who does not verbalize her love often, was beaming and has told me that I'm now such a free spirit, whereas before I was stressed and yelled a lot. I held them and apologized for all those times I flew away, and felt pressure to be someone else, to do more than love my people well, work appropriately hard, and try to enjoy my life. I'm thrilled that they recognize the shift and love this new version of me. More importantly, I love this version of myself too. And that's probably been one of the hardest but most rewarding parts about this journey: both building a life and a version of myself that I love, and then actively loving *her*. She was part of my bold vision, I just had no idea she was worth finding or how to get to her.

Gather Your Crew

Recall from the opening chapter, we are hardwired for connection. Having people around you who can understand or support your decision is crucial. Understanding what exactly that support looks like can be a little confusing. Make a list of people who will clap for you as you make these changes, who will spur you on when things get tough, who will encourage you to grow instead of focus your attention on the risks. Then really think about what type of support you'll need from each: weekly cheerleading, accountability texts monthly, opening their network to you for a new role, coaching or know-how about a different industry, insights into what your kids might need in the coming years so you know what to expect, financial support as you re-architect a career, kid coverage from a partner so that you can take that improv class and continue your growth, or just: listening to be heard and understood.

Gathering support for the changes you want to make is a key step, but it can be hard to execute. What is the best way to build a community with your crew; is it articulating the support you want and how you want it, and following up monthly? Joining an accountability group of like-minded women? Hosting your own monthly dinner to both get and give support to others? Asking for what you need periodically?

I made a commitment on my journey to be bolder in asking for the support I need, and have been surprised at how many people freely offered it. But there may be other surprises in exactly *who* offers that support. Look back at what you discovered in the Evaluate chapter around your patterns and the roles you take on in relationships. If you tend to be a people pleaser, if you look outside yourself for validation, if you play a certain role in your family or job like breadwinner or supporting cast, if you are surrounded by people who view the world in a polarized set of decisions where one path is wrong and the other is right, then this part could be hard. You're going to need to trust yourself, tell yourself you have enough information to make the right decision, acknowledge the role shift that you're making, and stay firm in your commitment to making a change.

One midwest entrepreneur, Nia, reminded me of the importance of life mentors in addition to work ones. As a working mother, having friends who were a few years older gave her and her husband a resource to anticipate their family changes as her own girls grew. I recently experienced this, as the women on my hockey team are ten years older than I am, with children of their own approaching college age. The advice they've given me spans from how to execute a hockey stop to how to navigate teenage emotions, and it's made me realize how important representation is in all walks of life.

Don't forget to include one very important member in your crew: your future self. That wise version of you who is living out your vision, who has healed from the past, and is enjoying the future life you envisioned for yourself. As odd as this sounds, you can look to her for guidance, and if you feel yourself pulled back into old patterns or at a decision crossroads, ask yourself: *What would my future self do?*

Chart a Course

For a lifelong planner, this is the fun part, putting all the pieces back together again in a plan to help you meet your own needs. We start with that purpose statement and make sure that everything else we decide to focus on ties back into that purpose. Debating an opportunity? Does it help you advance the purpose or distract you? Once you have the purpose outlined, we'll group the rest of the changes you want to make into three dimensions of what it takes to thrive as a leader: Mind, Body, and Spirit. The mind includes the head – career, calling, financial needs – while the body focuses more on physical and emotional needs, plus your environment. That leaves the spirit: social and relationships, fun and creativity, spirituality, growth and self-care.

How To Build

In our Evaluate chapter, you looked at patterns or mindsets to release, and in our Arise chapter, you focused on healthy habits to add into your life across the Mind, Body, and Spirit dimensions. Here's where you get to build a wishlist of all the activities you'd like to achieve across these dimensions:

Corporate Rehab Leadership © Dimensions

Mind
- Career & Calling *(vocation, job, passion)*
- Finances *(relationship with money, investments, needs, salary goals)*

Body
- Physical & Emotional *(fitness, physical wellness; mental & emotional health)*
- Environment & Energy *(what you surround yourself with; what gives vs. takes)*

Spirit
- Social & Relationships *(friends, romance, children, activities, community)*
- Fun & Creativity *(adventure, play, hobbies, sport)*
- Spirituality *(relationship with higher power; self-discovery)*
- Growth & Self-Care *(learning, certifications, education, pampering, self-nurturing)*

Looking at the mind dimension, you'll need to assess the logistics involved in making a change. Quitting sounds amazing, but you still need to eat, *right*? Most of us don't take the step of a sudden exit, followed by extreme insight and healing, and landing in a purpose-driven role that pays a great salary. You get to decide for yourself whether to make incremental changes or whether a full transformation is warranted. And you can heal and change the culture around you from right where you are. So, if the lessons to this point have resonated with you, *what are your options?*

This is the point at which you can revisit your old limiting beliefs and assess whether what you are telling yourself is indeed true. Michelle, an education reform executive, recalled a time when she knew she had to shift her role, but couldn't afford to quit. The process forced her and her husband to re-evaluate what they truly needed. She wound up staying a year longer than she wanted while she planned her exit and saved for the time she'd need to look for another job. Ask yourself:

- Financial Security: How much do I need to cover my cash flow and savings? How much do I want to be able to bring in, in order to finance the dreams I have, plus retirement and basic needs? Do I really have enough to live comfortably? Am I using money to fill an emptiness in my life or relationships, or avoid feeling vulnerable?

- Market Price: How much am I worth in the market? When was the last time I spoke to a recruiter and understood the market, and how much I should be asking for?

- Should I stay or should I go? Do I dread Monday mornings? Does the thought of work cause anxiety; a pit in my stomach or a tightness in my chest?

- What do I want from my life *right now*? Is it time to go back a few days a week so I have something that is mine, or time to get a bigger job and ask for that raise to put the kids through college, or time to say I've done enough?

Your next career steps could include staying within the role and changing it from the inside out, changing roles within the company, or becoming an entrepreneur. If you feel your soul dying slowly, it's time to eject. Pushing yourself harder in this moment won't fill the emptiness or make you feel like you are enough - only you can do that. Take a leave of absence, a sabbatical, or find a bridge job while you figure out your next steps.

If you can afford to wait a bit, time your exit taking into account the financial launchpad you'll need to take a job with a different hours/salary tradeoff, or to start your own thing. With my coaching clients, we build *Rehab Roadmaps* that chart out a 12-36 month timeline to make the changes outlined in this chapter more achievable.

Shifting over to the body, how will you sustain what you've learned in both physical and emotional wellbeing? And in your surrounding environment? One executive, Maya, decided to go cold turkey and quit her job suddenly, to take a yoga immersion class and then figure out next steps. Others told me about incremental changes they made, or had planned to quit until we walked through this process to detach from hustle culture and make intentional choices, and wound up staying with renewed purpose. One way to make these changes stick is to keep one small promise to yourself as you rebuild trust in your own decisions and career choices. I've started every day with prayer and journaling (including focusing on gratitude) for the last two years and it's reframed the day. To make it work, though, I had to give up keeping my phone on my nightstand, go back to a paper journal that helps me track both gratitude and my morning ritual, and institute a ten-minute break in the day in case I don't get to it in the morning. Instead of waking up anxious that my to-do list is already long and time is ticking, I acknowledge the anxiety and shift out of the frenzied pace into something a bit more manageable. The tasks are still there ten minutes later, but *I'm* different.

And, finally, spirit; how do you intend to keep growing in relationships, skills, adventure, spirituality, and your relationship with yourself? What boundaries do you need to place to protect your resources of time and energy? What can you do to protect your emotional and mental health in the presence of a toxic boss or friend? What will you commit to in self-care or even self-love? What did you fall in love with during the play section and want more of? Is it time to buy that trampoline?

Congrats! You've just invested the time to grow into a thriving leader, building new dimensions of your life and career. Now, you're ready to make some intentional decisions about which ladder to climb, or whether the corporate ladder itself needs to be reimagined.

CHAPTER 10

BUILDING A BETTER
BALANCE SHEET

*"If you choose not to decide. You still have
made a choice."*

— Rush

I t's one thing to lose yourself in your roles, mindsets, and old
behaviors. It's quite another to work in a company or culture
that forces you to *abandon* yourself to fit in. Healing and
thriving for yourself is the first step. *But what would it take to
rehab corporate America?*

First, we'd need to admit that this way of working...is no longer
working. As one retail executive, Bev, reminded me, "It shouldn't
take a cancer diagnosis to make us change our habits. But just like
we can't see a path out of the hustle culture for ourselves, leaders
can't see a way to stop driving so hard." *Her vision?* "Businesses
can be a force for good, led by strong and ethical humans creating
room for people to be fully human."

I'll just go ahead and say it, the thing that working women whisper
to each other all the time, like some precious insight we've found,
but feel guilty admitting: For many of us, it's *easier* to go to work

than to stay home and raise kids. There, *I said it*. We can break that down in a million ways, but the reality is that in modern America, you get paid and externally validated for the work you do inside the four walls of an office, but not for the work you do within the four walls of *your home.*

Both are extremely important, and I'm not here to debate your life choices and pit women against each other as if one is better than the other. That is a convenient argument to limit women to binary choices, instead of questioning *why* it is teed up as a binary choice in the first place. How convenient, to be presented with only two options, and then fight over which is better.

But the fact remains that, as a society, we place external value and compensation, defined as being included in GDP, on work *outside* the home, and little to no external value or compensation on the important work done inside it. That work is validated by your book club, by making memories in your Facebook posts, and echoed in the halls of churches, mosques, and synagogues across America, insisting that your place in the home is the only thing holding this country or your family together. And it may very well be.

Women have long been the society-builders, the church volunteers, the classroom moms. In my leafy DC neighborhood, which is mostly dual-income with two sizable careers, the carpool organizers and the camp dropper-offers are still ALWAYS the moms. What if we *did* value that work by paying women just minimum wage for the unpaid efforts they put into our American society? In 2020, women would have been paid $1.5 trillion.[106]

---

[106] Gus Wezerek and Kristen R. Ghodsee, *Women's Unpaid Labor is Worth $10,900,000,000,000,*, (NYTimes, March 5, 2020).

Many of those moms are working in a system that forces them to choose between work and the rest of their lives– but it only rewards them for the *work*. I found myself in a cycle where I struggled with work/life balance but the tyranny of the urgent always won. And, if I was honest with myself, I received zero credit for raising two small humans, and so many accolades for nailing a job presentation. The hit I got from producing work I was proud of, or the client or colleagues saying they 'couldn't have done it without me,' just wasn't the same as the satisfaction I felt from cooking a meal or driving my kids to events. And when life got hard, as it always does, it was tempting to say 'yes' when the options were "we really need you at this pitch" versus "clean toddler pee off the bathroom floor."

Asha, who left her IT role, shared how she felt when leaving the workforce to stay home with her two boys. "It's easy to feel like a failure because there's no tangible outcome...nothing that you can grasp. Your presence is ensuring the opposite of a negative outcome: you're keeping the family running."

If we want to live fuller lives, the way we *value* our lives has to change - which means the way we value our time has to change, and the way we value work must change. For those of us accustomed to the billable hour, this is not a foreign concept. Number of hours multiplied by rate equals value. But the items missing in that equation are quality instead of quantity, and impact. Intentional choices about what you spend your time on. Chasing fulfillment or happiness, alongside success. Not just time making memories, but time dedicated to adding value to something outside of the roles you play. Not just time landing big deals or running a company, but enjoying the life you've been working so hard to build. Time spent on filling yourself up so you don't rely on others to do it for you.

In studying what makes leaders thrive, several themes began to repeat: bold, authentic, empowering, relationships, connection, purpose, integrity, respect, passion, influence. The list wasn't about how much you dominate, control, or even how much action you take. It's a prescription for showing up as human. For not leaving behind some of the best parts of yourself when you walk into the office. Most of the traits align with what researcher and businesswoman Claire Zammit calls *The Divine Feminine*, and they stand in sharp contrast to what authors Nilima Bhat and Raj Sisodia of *Shakti Leadership* call the "wounded masculine" which they believe the business world has embraced. Scarcity instead of abundance, competition instead of collaboration, and overpowering others instead of empowering them.[107] Maybe there's a glaring reason these feminine leadership traits are largely missing from corporate America, or politics, or many of the places where decisions are made. **Women are missing from many of the places where decisions are made.**

If we want to truly shift out of surviving and into thriving, my research pointed to several common traits found in leaders and cultures who do thrive:

THRIVE *Model:*

Trust - build a culture of trust and the psychological safety to speak up

Help - ask for and receive help, and model vulnerability where needed

Respect - model respect and autonomy across levels of the organization

---

[107] Nilima Bhat and Raj Sisodia, *Shakti Leadership: Embracing Feminine and Masculine Power in Business* (Oakland, CA: Berrett-Koehler, 2016).

Impact - focus on your purpose, and connect it to the organization's purpose

Values - model integrity in living your values and authenticity to show up as yourself

Empathy - value connection with others and the role of emotion in the workplace

These seem like a good list of attributes, but we are in crisis mode for each of the elements required for thriving cultures and leaders. Trust has never been lower in the workplace, we are one of the only developed nations without national level support for working caregivers, and lack of respect and ethical values in work cultures drove the Great Resignation. Having a purpose-led company and empathy in leadership have resurfaced as buzzwords, yet 30% of employees today do not feel seen or heard at work.[108]

And, yet, each of these elements - Trust, Help, Respect, Impact, Values, Empathy - are traditionally feminine leadership traits. *You have everything you need within you*. Regardless of gender, we all have access to both masculine and feminine leadership styles; you just may have an advantage here if you happen to be a woman. We need more women leaders to show up as themselves and model these traits.

And we need more women in leadership.

Change yourself, and it will change the collective. By reconnecting with yourself, you're bringing forth your gifts and strengths that the world, your family, and the workforce desperately need. We have the opportunity for business to be a force for good in our lifetime. Value can be found in wealth and job creation, but also in

---

[108] *2022 State of Workplace Empathy Report*, Businessolver blog, page 7.

solving the world's most important problems. For you, that may be climate change, or social unrest, or products with purpose, or widespread trauma and mental illness. On an individual level, you get to decide what you value, including happiness and not just success, and then shift your life to make space for it. Not claim to be working so hard for your family, and then staying in a job that takes you away from them. Not saying you're in a role for the innovation, but really the steady paycheck is what keeps you hooked. Join a mission-focused company who lives out the values you cherish in your daily work. Get fulfillment from something outside of your career and let that joy spill over into all the interactions in your life. Start your own company or link up with another woman with twenty years of experience who is tired of outdated ways of leading, and make your own rules. Either way, YOU get to decide.

Greg McKeown has some fantastic advice on how to decide what stays and goes in his book, *Essentialism: The Disciplined Pursuit of Less*, focusing on three steps: explore, eliminate, and execute. He describes how to explore by discerning the trivial from the vital, to get to the right thing for the right reason at the right time. Next, cut out the trivial. The question, he says, is not how we can do it all, but *who* gets to choose what we do and don't do (spoiler alert: it's you). Finally, removing obstacles to make it happen, and taking action– quickly. He recalls the day of his daughter's birth, when a colleague asked him to attend a client meeting, and instead of applying these three lenses, he did what he thought he *should* do to please others: he attended the meeting hours after his daughter's birth. His client was actually dismayed at his choice, and he learned an important lesson: if you don't prioritize your life, someone else will.[109]

---

[109] Greg McKeown. *Essentialism, page 10.*

Ask yourself:

- What would it look like to bring all parts of yourself to work, and to home? To be a leader without losing yourself?

- What innovation could be unlocked if we truly treated people like the assets they are, getting the best from the brightest?

- What would it mean for businesses to be a force for good, rather than an afterthought or something nice to have?

- What decisions would we make if the executive floor was filled with diverse and thriving executives, in touch with their own power and gifts, and unafraid to apply those towards the world's toughest and most important problems?

Just stop for a second and picture it. What would it look like if C-suites across America were filled with executives who *expanded the definition of value and rewrote the rules of the game*? Who redefined sustainable growth, not as simply outsized returns on an income statement, but as the ability to grow both long-term results and purposeful impact, for individuals and their communities? An approach to winning that gave permission for its executives to be whole humans at work, not just racing to the top of a pyramid that is literally a man-made construct? What if decisions were made by executives who saw their role in driving revenue as inextricably linked to the importance of playing catch with their daughter after a long day? Their role as father teaching a son how to avoid toxic masculinity being just as important as their current title as a business titan? A system of working that was *designed* to work for all, not make accommodations for some to fit themselves into a game that many don't think needs changing.

I think that version of corporate America would be ridiculously profitable. For families raising the next generation of leaders, for societies currently in turmoil, and, yes, even for bank accounts.

All the data point towards balanced, diverse workplaces driving outsized financial returns, reducing turnover, driving more innovation. When business is a force for good, it's actually good for business.

Changing the collective could be as complicated as taking years to deconstruct societal norms and racial and gender bias. Or as simple as: start with you. Be a more humane leader in your own circle of influence. Change the compensation of those who report to you to ensure equity in pay. Model the behavior you want and leave on time. Thrive right where you are, and use your voice to impact others. But, remember, you may be up against a system that benefits mightily from you being a productive robot. If you want this to stick, there has to be a personal benefit and a communal monetary one. It has to make sense on multiple levels, so effortlessly that it just becomes natural. Human, *even*.

If corporations really are just groups of people agreeing to be bound by cultural norms, what are you doing to shape yours and redefine what you value? As an executive, as a leader, as an employee, as a parent? We can collectively decide that the old ways of allowing revenue to predominantly drive value are simplistically quaint, at best, and, at worst, disastrous to building innovation and healthy culture.

To truly rehab corporate America, it would require:

1. **Humane cultures** that reward productivity and respect; that balance masculine and feminine power; revenue and winning alongside creativity and collaboration.
2. Support infrastructure to provide **caregiving**– regardless of gender.
3. **Access to capital**, in both pay equity and equal access to investment funds.

4. Changes to the **balance of power** in your teams and in your home, from who takes the notes to who does the meal planning.

5. **Co-inventing corporate 2.0** with Gen Z or Gen A, right now. The Industrial Revolution was 200 years ago. It's time to retire productivity as the main measure.

This may sound like a revolution. But it's actually an *evolution*. We're just waking up to the fact that we're meant for more; we are designed to be connected with ourselves, asking for what we need, being present with our families while creating amazing things in our work. I used to worry I wasn't the right person to share this message; I'm the privileged white cis woman who was successful by many measures inside of the system I write about. But maybe I'm exactly the right person. I've been inside these C-suites, I'm friends with the people who run them, I'm married to a white man, I was the poster child for hustle culture, I am currently raising children, and I intimately remember my own experience in juggling roles. I leaned *all the way in*, until I realized that was only part of the equation. I've been on the inside and benefitted from the power structure, and seen enough to know where it needs to evolve. Maybe we have to crack the facade of the hustle culture in order for new growth to shoot up through the cracks in the pavement.

I don't have all of the answers to what will work best for you. *But you do.* You just may not know it yet. Right now, there's a flicker of an idea in the back of your mind about how you could start this today, in your team, in your family, in your community. There will be a million reasons why it won't work. There will be mindsets and behaviors that will need to shift. You will have people in your life who will not want to join you on this journey. Others who will shame you for even asking for change. Focus on the vision of what could be, in the world and in your own life, and why things must change. *Why not you?* You wouldn't be having these thoughts or have picked up this book if some part of your soul wasn't looking for answers.

In my work and life, I had always wished for a wise woman a few years ahead of me – first in my husband's residency and then in my own partnership path – to help me navigate these decisions. It took the world getting quiet for me to realize: I am who I was waiting for. And so are you. Go do your own *Corporate Rehab* and build a better way for yourself, your family and your teams, and change the rules for corporate America as you go. I'm cheering you on.

ACKNOWLEDGEMENTS

I am so grateful for all the people who helped this book come into the world.

To the women I interviewed, so many of whom required anonymity for fear of reprisal or because of the sensitive nature of their stories, thank you for trusting me to bring these into the light.

To my colleagues and friends who reached out with support when I left my job, encouraging me to keep speaking the truth and share their stories, thank you. To the bosses who inspired and supported me by being extremely human leaders, and to those who championed a leadership style or life I no longer wanted, you each played a role in getting me to this place. To my fellow female partners, I love and respect you so very much and have been in your shoes - please know that I'm cheering you on.

To my editing team at Authority Coach including Jeremy Jones, my initial writing mentor and group including Eric Koester at the Creators Institute, my developmental editor Betsy Allen, book coach Martha Bullen, amazing PR team at Nardi Media my Beta reader team Kelly, Frederique, Colston, Sindhu, Julia, and my cover stylist, Laiz. Thank you for all your patience through all the iterations and changes.

To all of my sisters at Chief - your community and support has been tremendous! I hope this book helps you and your teams reach the C–suite if that is your chosen path, launch companies, and be leaders in your own lives.

To my friends who supported me by checking in or making introductions, especially my UVA girls, Kelly, Sarah, Jess and Shelley, and my DC crew who stepped up in so many ways from dropping off writing notebooks, to offering suggestions on morning runs to championing the book and quotes on LinkedIn that you loved - you know you are and I'm so grateful, Anita, Lori, Maribeth, Athena, Liz, and so many others.

To my original crew, my parents, who gifted me the hustle and grit that earned me more opportunities and options than I could have imagined, and my two grandmothers, who did the best they could. And to my twin sister, my first protector and partner, for your love throughout the years and the opportunity to grow together in this next chapter.

Finally, I'd like to forever thank my family: Kevin, Jackson and Avery. Your support and enthusiasm has been crucial as we rediscover what we're meant to do together in this world. You've each grown right alongside me on this journey, and that has been a gift I do not take lightly. Kevin, you are the bravest man I know, and I cannot wait to see what you do next. I'll be right here, cheering you on.

AUTHOR BIO

After spending 20 years in Corporate America helping Fortune 500 leadership companies manage multi-million dollar growth strategies, Jennie left her partnership in a global consulting firm to launch her own company. In addition to her role as CEO, she also serves as a professional speaker, an Adjunct Professor in Strategy, a Board member, and the author of Corporate Rehab: ditch the hustle culture and thrive again.

Her coaching and speaking business focuses on female executives looking to reach the next level of leadership without losing themselves in the process, and on companies interested in building human-centered cultures. She lives in Washington, DC with her husband, two kids, and Labrador puppy, and is trying to enjoy this chance to rewrite the next chapter of her career and life by running 10 milers, learning poetry, and playing ice hockey.